His Wonders in the DEEP

Inkwell Heritage Publishing

18896 Greenwell Springs Road
Greenwell Springs, LA 70739

His Wonders in the DEEP

God's Call to the Supernatural

by

Andrea "Andy" McDougal

His Wonders in the Deep

Unless otherwise noted, all Scriptures references are from the Amplified Bible, copyright © 1987 by the Zondervan Corporation and the Lockman Foundation, La Habra, California. References marked KJV are from the Authorized King James Version of the Bible. The quotes marked as Strong's" are from *Strong's Exhaustive Concordance of the Bible With Greek and Hebrew Dictionaries* by James Strong (Dugan Publishers, Inc.: Gordonsville, Tennessee, no date). Quotes marked as from "Young's" are from *The Analytical Concordance to the Bible by Robert Young* (Eerdmans Publishing Company: Grand Rapids, Michigan, no date). Word definitions are taken from the following dictionaries: *Webster Seventh New Collegiate Dictionary, The New Lexicon Webster's Dictionary, Jones' Dictionary of Old Testament Proper Names, Webster's Unabridged Second Edition Deluxe* and *World Book Dictionary*.

Published by:

Inkwell Heritage Publishing
18896 Greenwell Springs Road
Greenwell Springs, LA 70739

ISBN: 979-8-9987460-1-7

Printed on demand in the US, the UK, and Australia
For Worldwide Distribution

Contents

Some go down to the sea and travel over it in ships to do business in great waters; these see the works of the Lord and HIS WONDERS IN THE DEEP.

Psalm 107:23-24

When He had stopped speaking, He said to Simon (Peter), Put out into the deep [water] and lower your nets for a haul.   Luke 5:4

Launch out into the deep.   KJV

About the Title

The principle scripture the Lord gave me for the writing of this book was Psalm 107:24, as you have already seen on the facing page. If I may paraphrase that verse here: "Those who go down to the sea and do business in great waters, these shall see the works of the Lord and His wonders in the deep." In other words, "Those who do God's business in deep waters shall see the wonders of the Lord."

You may be thinking, "What exactly is a 'wonder'?" This is what I call an intangible word. A wonder, as described in *Strong's Analytical Concordance*, is "something great and wonderful; the hidden things of God that are so high they are out of our earthly reach." A wonder is "a miracle." It is "the miraculous workings of God that are Heaven-sent and that bring about the much needed miracles in our lives and the lives of those around us." It is the wondrous works of the Lord that, at times, seem as if they are hidden from us! A "wonder" will always bring glory to the Lord, but, in the process, will also help to bring you into greater works and a greater level of ministry.

"His wonders," then, are manifestations of His Presence or, should I say, a revealing or uncovering of His Presence or of Himself to us, His people. When these "wonders" begin to happen in our lives, it increases our faith to believe Him for the next great miracle. "His wonders" will always lead or point us to the Lord and His Kingdom. They will cause the lost to repent and to receive Christ as Lord and Savior.

But, as stated in Psalm 107:24, it is when we are doing the business of the Kingdom or the work of the Lord in *"great [deep] waters"* that we will see and experience the wonders of Heaven, not when we remain in shallow water or on the fringe of where the Lord wants to take us. It is when we stand in the deep waters of His Spirit that we will experience those miraculous things that have been, up until now, out of our reach. It is then that we experience the fullness of the Kingdom of God in the earth!

In the title, we not only have the words *His Wonders,* but we also have *in the Deep.* When Luke, the disciple of Jesus, wrote (in the book that bears his name) that Jesus told him and the other disciples to *"launch out into the deep"* (Luke 5:4), that word *deep* means "mysteries, deep things, the profound things of God." It means going far deeper than what is understood. *Strong's* also states that the word *deep* means "profundity," which speaks of not only profound things, but a place that is very deep indeed.

This is the abyss, and another word for *abyss* is *Hell*. Let me state it like this: the deep or the abyss is the sea of humanity, far too many of which are living lives of darkness, a veritable Hell on earth, without the true and living God. Unless you and I go to them and lead them into His Kingdom (in other words, if we never *"launch out into the deep,"*) we will never see the lost come to Christ and come out of the abyss, and we will also never see the profound mysteries of the Kingdom. So this word *deep* has a double meaning: It means to be launched into the sea of humanity to bring in a harvest, and it also means to be launched into the mysteries, or the deep and profound things of God.

When you launch out into the *deep*, a deeper revelation of the Christ and of His Word will come to you. Onion-skin layers that have hidden the truths of that Word will be pulled back, and those truths will be revealed or unveiled. But there will also be a great harvest, and you will then be able to impact the world around you by bringing those who are in darkness into God's marvelous light. This, then, is what we mean by *His Wonders in the Deep*.

Author's Preface

While I was writing this book, I had the privilege of visiting the Smithsonian National Museum of Natural History located in our nation's capital. I loved many of the displays I saw there that day, but one of them spoke to me more profoundly than others. It was an exhibit concerning the vast, as-yet-unexplored deepest parts of the world's oceans.

This unique presentation was prepared by the scientists of the Woods Hole Oceanographic Institute in Massachusetts. These scientists reported that they felt very privileged to be able to do deep underwater exploration because every time they went down they were able to see and photograph things never before seen by any human. Their description of some of the creatures of the deep was breathtaking.

These never-before-seen creatures, they reported, have the ability to give off what they call bioluminescence, or chemical light, in many beautiful colors. So, as the scientists descended into the darkness of the deep ocean places, a very special light show began, and they were the only ones privileged to see it. And this, they contend, is just the beginning. As men are able to go deeper and deeper into the unexplored areas of the world's seas, many more discoveries await. Isn't it exciting! There are worlds that we don't yet know of just waiting for us to discover.

As I watched a video presentation of what these scientists had witnessed, I could not help but relate it to the glory of God that is so beautifully displayed these days as we step into deeper waters. There is a color, a luminescence, and a beauty that is not available to man's common shallow levels of experience, but can only be known in the greater depths. I pray that through the words of this book you may be challenged to search out and find *His Wonders in the Deep.*

Introduction

I don't know about you, dear reader, but there came a moment in my life when I suddenly grew tired of shallow waters and felt an unmistakable and strong calling to the deeper places in God. In fact, I have discovered that the voice of the Father, indeed His very heartbeat, is urging us all deeper these days.

It's time for rivers to swim in. It's time to get out of the ankle-deep water, the knee-deep water and the loin-deep water, for this is a new day, the day of the Lord's harvest, a time of critical reaping. It's time to get serious with God, to mean business with Him, to launch out into the deep places with Him. There's no time to lose.

When David said, *"Some go down to the sea and travel over it in ships to do business in great waters,"* the people of his day traveled long distances in great ships, while today we might fly, drive or take a train or bus. The important thing is not the particular mode of transportation, but doing business in "great waters" or "in the deep."

This passage does not necessarily indicate that we will all travel great distances in the future for God. Some will, while others will be engaged in serious business for Him and His Kingdom right in their own neighborhoods. Some will go to other cities, and some will surely go to other countries, for the Lord's harvest fields are vast. But wherever our call might take us in the days ahead, the important thing is that we each get into some deep waters and in those deep waters do some serious business on behalf of God's Kingdom.

Why is getting into deeper water so important? It's important because it's when we get into deeper waters that God begins to manifest His glory in our lives. When we begin to swim in His deeper waters, that's when we begin to see *"His wonders."* Those who choose to stay in the shallows will never see the greater things, for the greater things of God are reserved for the deep.

Some people are afraid of the unknown, and the thought of going deeper frightens them. But I promise you that if you'll answer God's call to the deep, you'll suddenly find yourself experiencing His presence and Kingdom in a new way.

In this important day in which we live, the Lord is searching for willing vessels, those whom He can empower and use. If you decide to be one of those who hear and respond to His call, He will thrust you out quickly into the deep places, and you will find yourself able to survive and thrive there in the depths.

Don't be afraid of deeper water, for God will never leave you there alone. He will surely care for you in the deep. Indeed, in the deep, you will experience His love as never before. That love will be revealed to you in a new measure. Yield to what God is doing, and you will quickly experience Him in a new way.

So launch out, for God has not called you to .a knee-deep experience. He cannot be pleased if you settle for the loin-deep water. His will for you is that you become totally immersed in the life-giving flow of His river.

Go ahead. Get on out into the deeper waters, and there you will begin to *see ... His wonders,* for when we begin doing business in great waters, we see many new and unique manifestations of God's glory and power.

So what are we waiting for? Let's move on out and experience *His Wonders in the Deep.*

Andrea "Andy" McDougal
Baton Rouge, Louisiana

My own launching forth into the deep came about because of a prophetic word given to me by the late Ruth Ward Heflin. For any who were not privileged to know this godly woman, she was a powerful servant of the Lord indeed.

The particular prophetic word of which I speak came to me through Ruth while I was attending a conference in Pass Christian, Mississippi, where she was ministering. Our encounter did not seem to take place under ideal circumstances, but God always knows best in these things. I had been accidentally locked out of my hotel room that day by a friend, with whom I was sharing the room, and my irritation over that situation was not conducive to hearing from God or of having a life-changing experience. Still, by the grace of God, it happened.

Because I was locked out, I was late for the service, and I was rushing up a flight of steps when I suddenly stumbled upon Ruth, and thus I stumbled into my destiny. That may sound strange to some, so allow me to explain.

There will be times in each of our lives when we just seem to "stumble" into the plans and purposes of God for our future. We haven't been expecting it, because we haven't known what to expect. We haven't been hoping for it or believing for it, because we haven't known exactly what to hope for or exactly what to believe for. But from one step to the next, we suddenly "stumble" into the Lord's plan, and we suddenly know His greater purposes for our lives. It is always a remarkable experience, and that day was no exception.

It was a hot September day, and it seemed to be filled with far too many irritations. Because of this, I could not have possibly realized that I was about to have such a profound and life-changing experience.

As I came face to face with Ruth Heflin that day, it was not my first encounter with her. Over the years, I had several times experienced what seemed to be chance encounters with this great woman, and each time my life was changed in some way. To have an encounter with Ruth Heflin was to have an encounter with God.

We had barely greeted each other this particular day when she laid her hands on me and began to prophesy many great things over my life. Among the amazing things she said that day was that I would be traveling to Israel within the next two weeks, all expenses paid, and that I would be staying with her in her home in Jerusalem.

It happened just as Ruth had spoken it. Two weeks later, I found myself, Along with Victoria Comeaux, a dear friend, at Ben Gurion International Airport in Tel Aviv. A rental car was waiting for us. We spent the night in Tel Aviv and drove up to Jerusalem the next morning. We would be there for the Feast of Tabernacles and would be staying in the home of Ruth Heflin, exactly as she had foreseen.

It was my first time to visit Israel, and I marveled at every vista, every sound, and every nuance, from my touchdown at the airport, to my trip up to Jerusalem and, later, my visit to the Galilee with my friend and traveling companion, Victoria.

And then it was on to other places around the country. It was a great adventure that my heart had long contemplated, and I found myself feeling like a little child, wanting to see everything there was to see and do everything there was to do.

While in the Galilee, we visited every place we could possibly get to. There was lunch in Tiberias, and then we went on to Capernaum, the Mount of Beatitudes, and many other holy places. It was all a wonderful delight to my soul. All the varied sights and sounds and impressions rushed in upon me, and I struggled to take it all in.

But, as exciting and wonderful as it was to be in that great land, I was soon to understand that the Lord had orchestrated our trip in a way that went beyond anything I could have imagined. He had sent me so far to His own homeland, to give me a revelation of His Word, a revelation that was to bring me to a new level of understanding and my ministry into an entirely new realm of anointing. It was this revelation that would eventually lead to the writing and publication of this book.

I was about to see my destiny stretched out before me in a new way. How amazing it was to me that the Lord would send me halfway around the world so that He could drop a new truth into my spirit, a truth I could share with others and see their lives and ministries changed as well. I was about to be launched out into the deep.

When our first day in the Galilee seemed to be coming to a close, the one regret I had was that we had not yet been able to take a Jesus boat and go out onto the sea. This seemed to be the practice of all believers who visited the Galilee. In fact, several times that day, locals asked us, "Have you been out on a Jesus boat on the sea?" We hadn't, and I was disappointed, for I had wanted very much to do that.

Within seconds of my voicing this disappointment, the Lord spoke to us through Psalm 107:23-24, *"Some go down to the sea and travel over it in ships to do business in great waters; these see the works of the Lord and His wonders in the deep."* I knew instantly that we would be on the Sea of Galilee before the night was over. But was that even possible? It was growing dark. Would there be night trips?

We were in Tiberias, and we began to inquire about any boats that might be going out on the lake that night. We were told that such a boat would be coming, and before long, we began to see its lights approaching over the water. I rushed off to buy our tickets for the boat trip, and my friend rushed off to buy some bread and juice so that we could share communion on the boat. It was a common practice for visitors to the Galilee to go on a "Jesus boat" and have communion on the sea, and we wanted to experience it too.

When my turn came to buy the tickets, the agent asked me if I understood that this was a "disco" boat. I wasn't sure what he meant by that, but we wanted to go out on the sea so badly that I was willing to risk whatever it was. Any kind of boat was all right with me, as long as we could be on the Galilee. Much to our surprise, we soon found ourselves onboard a boat with a group of people ready to dance the night away. And there we were, two sheltered Pentecostal/ Charismatic ladies, eager to share together our holy communion at sea.

At first, it seemed like we had made a gigantic mistake, but we hadn't. That night, as we shared the boat with a worldly group that cared nothing for what Jesus had done there, in what (to us) was a very holy place, a revelation of the lost seeking the deep began to sweep over my soul. We were sharing communion with the lost in the deep, and the whole purpose of the deep, the Lord was showing me, was to fulfill the heartcry of the Father for the lost. We were going out to the deep, surrounded by the world.

Here we were on the Sea of Galilee, one of the deepest spots on the face of the earth, and we were on a disco boat filled with people dancing and partying. The King of Glory, the Great I Am, the One who held my life, my destiny and my purpose in the palm of His hands, had ordered my footsteps around to the other side of the world, to give me a revelation of His Word, a revelation of the deep.

I found it to be a wonderfully exhilarating experience. I was not just reading the Bible and doing some nice word study. I was experiencing firsthand the reality of the Word of God and the impact it was intended to make upon the world around us. I was experiencing the call of God to a new level.

In previous years, I had served as a missionary to Mexico and was blessed to win a multitude of souls into the Kingdom, but now a greater depth of ministry was being made available to me.

This was profound. Even though I had laid on my face many times through the years answering a new level of the call of God upon my life, I had never answered His call under such strange circumstances. I was being taken into the deep, and I knew that I was about to see the wonders of God in new ways.

I had no idea how deep "deep" was to be, and I didn't fully understand how wonderful the wonders would be that God would soon manifest in my life and ministry. What I was sensing was that I was getting into some deeper waters, waters that I could swim in, and the thrill of it consumed me.

Before we move on, there is one more thing I must tell you about the disco boat. The music they played that night was in Arabic or Hebrew, and we didn't understand a word of it. Then, suddenly, a song began to play, but this time in English.

Just weeks before going to Israel I had been teaching a series on the book of Esther. She was a woman who came from obscurity, found favor with the king, and had an amazing rise to royal estate. During my studies, I found that the crown she wore was tall, shaped like a chef's hat of today, and was reminiscent of a stove pipe. For this reason, it was called a "chimney."

Now we were on the deepest part of the sea. and total darkness surrounded us, except for the lights of the disco boat. The lights of Tiberias and the shoreline of the Galilee could hardly be seen. We had just finished having communion on the deep in the midst of the world and had yielded our lives to God's call, when the English song was heard. (Incidentally, all of the young women aboard the boat were dressed in long, flowing gowns, and each wore a glistening crown upon her head.)

Now the English words rang out, and I was amazed at what I heard. Over and over the artist sang, "What would she look like with a chimney on her head." "What would she look like with a chimney on her head." "What would she look like with a chimney on her head." I was immediately drawn back to the teaching on Queen Esther, a type of the Bride of Christ, a deliverer of God's people and the Esthers who were currently being birthed in the earth, *"for such a time as this,"* a true Bride for Christ and one who will know and experience the depths of the Kingdom of God. Esther's life was miraculous from beginning to end, and she experienced *His Wonders in the Deep.*

The next evening after that boat ride on the Galilee we found ourselves at the Dead Sea. In a strange way, it was the same water as we had seen in the Galilee. The water of the Sea of Galilee flows out through the Jordan River, and the Jordan River eventually winds its way downward into the Dead Sea. And just as the waters continued to flow, the revelation continued. As we were leaving the Dead Sea that evening, another unusual thing happened that further deepened my understanding of what God was showing me.

A little Bedouin man began to speak to me in English, and I was shocked, not only at how he said it, but also at what he said. The man had never seen me before, nor did he know anything about what the Lord was showing and teaching me. Yet when he saw me, the first words out of his mouth were these: "Do you know how deep the Dead Sea is? Do you know how deep the Sea of Galilee is?" When I indicated that I didn't know the answer, he went on: "Well, the Galilee is one of the deepest spots on the earth, but as the water of the Jordan flows down from there to the Dead Sea, it goes even deeper. This is the deepest spot on Earth."

When I was able to look all of this up, I found that the man was absolutely right. The Sea of Galilee (also known as Kinneret, Lake of Gennesaret, or Lake Tiberias) is a very unique body of water. It is not a sea at all, but rather a fresh-water lake, the largest in Israel. It is 13 miles long and 8 miles wide and is fed partly by underground springs, but its main source of water is the Jordan River that actually flows through it, entering at the north end of the lake and exiting at the south end. The lake is about 140 feet deep, but it sits at 700 feet below sea level, making it the lowest (or deepest) fresh-water lake on Earth and the second-lowest (or deepest) lake overall (after the Dead Sea, which is a saltwater lake).

As the Jordan exits the Sea of Galilee it continues to wind its way downward, ever deeper, until it empties into the Dead Sea, also called the Salt Sea or The Sea of Death. Again, this is not a sea at all, but a salt-water lake. Parts of the Dead Sea have a depth of more than 1,200 feet. But whereas the Sea of Galilee is 700 feet below sea level, the shores of the Dead Sea sit at nearly 1,400 feet below sea level and then the slopes plunge on down from there. This is, therefore, the deepest body of water on the Earth, and the area around the lake is Earth's lowest (or deepest) elevation on land. The Dead Sea is 34 miles long and 11 miles wide and at 1,237 feet deep, is also the deepest hypersaline lake in the world and one of the saltiest (8.6 times saltier than the ocean).

That little Bedouin man and I had been able to speak for only a short time that day, but as we went our way, I was convinced that the Lord had used him, a man from the other side of the world, to confirm the revelation He was trying to give me. As for me, I had gotten the message. God was speaking to me about deep places in Him and a deep anointing that would minister to those trapped in the deep darkness of sin.

When we eventually left Israel, these words would be indelibly imprinted upon my heart: *"Some go down to the sea and travel over it in ships to do business in great waters."* I had come to this sacred land by air, but I was conscious of having done some serious business in great waters. And now I knew the promise: *"These shall see the works of the Lord and HIS WONDERS IN THE DEEP."* When we do business in deep waters with God, we are destined to see His wonders.

As the days turned into weeks, the weeks into months, and the months into years, I would begin to know the wonders of God in a new and glorious way. God would begin opening the windows of Heaven over my life and causing me to understand the revelation of the times in which we were living and our destined place in His vast vineyard. Clearly, my life was about to be turned upside down, and I would never be the same again.

Within a few days of returning home from Israel, I was again boarding a plane, this time for Jamaica. A few ladies who were involved in my ministry were accompanying me on a mission to that country. I had preached several times before in Kingston, but this time our friends who were hosting the meetings I would be speaking in took us to the north part of the island, to a town known as Ocho Rios (Eight Rivers). Much to our surprise, we were to stay in a beautiful private resort on the shore of the Caribbean Sea. What a lovely setting it was, but to me it was more than the natural beauty of the place. I again sensed that God was speaking to me. Here we were on the shores of deep water — again.

When I went into the main cabana, my eyes fell on the title of a book strategically placed on a coffee table in the living room. It said THE DEEP. My heart leaped!

Outside there was a lovely concrete balcony surrounded by concrete railings, and we could sit there and view the water, or we could actually descend and walk along the beach if we wanted.

Another part of the property, reserved for newly-married couples, was called The Bridal

Suite, It was a small apartment built under the concrete balcony and right at the shore line of the sea. It had a door and windows looking out onto the sea. The thing that really got my attention was that at high tide the waves from the Caribbean, the waves of the deep, would actually roll up over the top of the suit, crashing against the windows and door. This spoke to me of the Bride of Christ and her relationship to the deep. Every day, it seemed, there were new and exciting confirmations that I was about to experience a new level of ministry.

What about you, dear friend? Has God's Spirit been calling you deeper? If so, please allow Him to minister to you through the pages of this book. You, too, are destined to see *His Wonders in the Deep.*

Chapter 1

The Clarion Call

In those days there appeared John the Baptist, preaching in the Wilderness (Desert) of Judea, and saying, Repent (think differently: change your mind, regretting your sins and changing your conduct), for the kingdom of heaven is at hand. This is he who was mentioned by the prophet Isaiah when he said, The voice of one crying in the wilderness [shouting in the desert], Prepare the road for the Lord, make His highways straight (level, direct).   Matthew 3:1-3

We must begin this book with Jesus, for He is not only our example; He is our Source, and all life flows out from Him. The ministry our Lord performed on earth for a few short years was handed down to us when He left, and His ministry to the world is now our ministry to the world. Because His coming into the world and what that meant to the world was so important, it was heralded in a very strange and powerful way.

The Unique Call

Just before Jesus began His ministry, a clarion-like voice, distinct in sound (a particular sound that had never before been heard by the people of that day), began to resound throughout all of Judea. It rang so loud and so clear that it pierced the very hearts of humanity. It shook the earth beneath the feet of those who heard it, and they were moved to respond with great abandonment. This voice, this sound coming from the wilderness, would soon bring a new paradigm into the earth. The Scriptures record:

> *Then Jerusalem and all Judea and all the country round about the Jordan went out to him {John}: and they were baptized in the Jordan by him, confessing their sins.*
>
> Matthew 3:5-6

Can you imagine it? This was monumental. Something that had never been seen before was coming into the earth. There was something on the horizon that had never been known to mankind before. The world was about to shake with the entrance of a new way of thinking, a new way of acting, and a new way of believing.

How blessed John was, for he was chosen to declare this coming event. His voice, *"the voice of one crying in the wilderness,"* was sent into the world to prepare the way for the earth-changing events that would now follow.

THE CALL FOR TOTAL CHANGE

The sound that was going forth throughout the land required the people of that day to begin to examine their lives and to *"repent,"* meaning to change the direction in which they were going. It required that they regret the errors of their past, change their minds, and adopt a totally new mode of behavior. There was to be nothing cosmetic about this change that God was requiring. It was to be a total change of heart and of mind.

His ministry to the world is now our ministry to the world!

3

This total change of heart and mind was also an irrevocable condition for receiving what was to come. An explosion of the Kingdom of God and its ministry to the earth was on the horizon, and only those who made room for it in their lives (agreeing not only to receive it, but also to act upon it) could participate.

Our New Call

The reason all of this excites me so much is that today we are again hearing an unusual sound coming forth from the heavens. This new sound is also clear and distinct, and it is echoing throughout the nations. This modern-day clarion call has reached the heart of many already, and they have begun to echo it to others.

As each of us receives this new call, we become a voice crying in the wilderness of our modern world, and we are now preparing the way for the entrance of God's Kingdom that will come to us in new power in these final hours of time. We have made ourselves the pathway, the highway, through which the Kingdom of Heaven will be released to all mankind.

What could possibly be more exciting? I trust that you will sense in the Spirit what is happening in these days and also that you will become excited enough about it to get on board and become part of it. Hear God's clarion call to you today.

THE ULTIMATE PLAN

In the case of John the Baptist, the Kingdom was not long in appearing:

> *Then Jesus came from Galilee to the Jordan to John to be baptized by him. But John protested strenuously, having in mind to prevent Him, saying, It is I who has need to be baptized by You, and do You come to me? But Jesus replied to him, Permit it just now; for this it the fitting way for [both of] us to fulfill all righteousness [that is, to perform completely whatever is right]. Then he permitted Him.*
> *And when Jesus was baptized, He went up at once out of the water; and behold, the heavens were opened, and he {John} saw the Spirit of God descending like a dove and alighting on Him. And behold, a voice from heaven said, This is My Son, My Beloved, in Whom I delight!*   Matthew 3:13-17

John had known all along that he was nothing more than a voice preparing the way for the rule of a new authority that would come after him. He knew that there was a greater

> The portals of the Kingdom were opened over God's Son, and great glory was suddenly descending upon the scene!

One to come, One filled with the power of Heaven. And when that One came (in the person of Jesus, the Christ, the Anointed One), John was quick to recognize Him.

The Baptism of Jesus

When Jesus first suggested to John that He, too, be baptized, John resisted the idea. Baptizing the Son of God didn't make any sense to him. Jesus, however, knew the plans of Heaven, and He knew that Heaven's wishes must be fulfilled. In the end, John realized that, despite his misgivings, he must yield to the greater plan and purpose of God. And so it was that Jesus went down into the waters of the Jordan to be baptized by His cousin John.

No sooner had John placed Jesus in the waters of the Jordan than the heavens were opened, and the Holy

Spirit, in the form of a dove, descended and lighted upon Jesus. The portals of the Kingdom were opened over God's Son, and great glory was suddenly descending upon the scene. God Himself spoke from Heaven and declared: *"This is My Son, My Beloved, in Whom I delight!"* (Matthew 3:17).

The Bible does not state what Jesus may have prayed in that moment, what words He may have uttered, as Heaven opened over Him, but since the purpose of this event was to release the new power and authority of Kingdom ministry into the world, He might have uttered the words which He would later teach His disciples to pray:

Our Father Who is in heaven, hallowed (kept holy) be Your name. Your Kingdom come, Your will be done on earth as it is in heaven.
Matthew 6:9-10

The Heavens Are Opened

Although the Bible does not describe in detail all that transpired in those moments, we know that the great I Am yielded to His Father's will, and Heaven opened as a result. In that moment, God's Kingdom and all that it represented began to flood down through the portals of Heaven and was released into the earth. The authority of

God, His will and purpose for mankind and His plan for all humanity began to be seen in a new way. At the very uttering of His words, the skies opened and the benefits of the Kingdom flowed into the earth.

The call of the Father's Kingdom was upon Jesus, and His mission was set before Him. He had come to do the will of His Father who had sent Him:

> *Then said he, Lo, I come to do thy will, O God.* Hebrews 10:9, KJV

These very words may well have been on Jesus' lips that day, as He totally surrendered to the powers of Heaven and committed Himself to the work ahead. It was a pregnant moment, for the earth would soon see *His Wonders in the Deep.*

CHAPTER 2

GREAT TESTINGS ALWAYS PRECEDE PROMOTION

Then Jesus was led (guided) by the [Holy] Spirit into the wilderness (desert) TO BE TEMPTED (TESTED AND TRIED) by the devil.   Matthew 4:1

Jesus' ministry was not to begin without a great test. Trials will always precede spiritual elevation. Paul, the great apostle, knew this all too well. He wrote:

For a wide door of opportunity for effectual [service] has opened to me [there, a great and promising one], and [there are] many adversaries.   1 Corinthians 16:9

Just before there is a release of a new level of ministry, we can usually expect a great onslaught of opposition!

Paul understood that every time he endeavored to go through any gate, into a more effective ministry, into a higher level of anointing, he would be opposed. This word *adversaries* that he used is defined by *Strong's* as "to lie opposite, be adverse, be contrary, to oppose" (*Strong's* #480). Our adversary is opposed to God's Kingdom, and when we begin to move with that Kingdom, we can expect to be opposed by him.

When we move with God, His adversaries become our adversaries. The forces that are contrary to His plans and purposes now array themselves against *us* — all because we have chosen to work to bring about heavenly plans and purposes.

Just before there is a release of a new level of ministry, we can usually expect a great onslaught of opposition. It will often come in the form of trials and testings.

Suddenly things that we never expected to face will stand boldly before us and challenge us. For instance, temptations that we have never faced in the past and never expected to face in the future will suddenly assail us. We will find ourselves in an unexpected battle for our very souls, and the greater the ministry at stake, the greater these attacks may become.

CHARGED WITH THE POWER OF HEAVEN

Jesus had come to the earth, and His ministry was about to come forth with great power and glory. It would be a ministry charged with the power of Heaven and accompanied with great signs and wonders. As a result, despite the fact that He was the very Son of God, He could not escape the tests He must face in those moments. Suddenly, therefore, the tempter was upon Him.

It is important to note that it was the Holy Spirit who led Jesus into the wilderness to face the adversary. God the Father knew what was taking place with His Son. He knew that Jesus was about to be tempted, tested and tried by Satan himself. It was inevitable.

TWO KINGDOMS ON A COLLISION COURSE

Jesus (God made manifest, God revealed in the flesh, God in the form of a man) had come

3

to earth. He was the true and living God, and He was coming as King and bringing with Him His Kingdom. He was about to institute a new order for the operation of His heavenly Kingdom and for the release of its authority throughout the earth. What had been purposed in Heaven from the foundations of the world was about to be revealed.

Just as Christ had come, the Kingdom of Heaven would now come with all its operations. Now the ministry of that new Kingdom, a Kingdom not of this world, would suddenly explode into the earth. When it happened, the lives of many who had been held prisoner by the forces of an opposing kingdom, a kingdom of darkness and ruthless destruction, would be set free.

What a moment! Heaven and the very things of Heaven were waiting to be released into the earth. The very purposes of God, held in reserve until this appropriate time, were about to be set on a collision course against the kingdoms of this world. A ministry of miracles without limitations or boundaries was now being thrust into the earth by the coming of the Lord Jesus Christ.

From the moment this new Kingdom power entered the earth's atmosphere and was seen by men, it began to collide with every opposing faction, and now a decisive battle was set up that would decide the final outcome.

THE CLASH OF OPPOSING KINGDOMS

Throughout history, when two opposing kingdoms have faced each other, there has always come an unavoidable showdown. Two opposing kingdoms cannot coexist and share authority within the same territory. There can be only one ruler, one king, and when two opposing kingdoms are determined to rule the same area, a clash of wills always ensues.

In the end, one of the opposing rulers must always come forth as victor, and he will then rule. The battle that was about to take place in the life of Jesus was to be no different. For the next forty days, the kingdom of darkness would throw everything it had at Him in an attempt to abort the coming of the Kingdom of God and its purposes in the earth.

In other ways, this was a whole new kind of battle. Suddenly a kingdom that was not of this world had come against all the existing kingdoms of the world, and the outcome would determine whom men served in the future. Everything opposed to God and to His Kingdom was suddenly arrayed against one person — Jesus of Nazareth. He must face everything that was adverse to and in contradiction to the plans and purposes of God, and He must overcome it all. When we speak of Jesus, therefore, as a

Victor, we must know that He valiantly earned His Victor's crown.

Now Jesus Could Begin His Ministry

Only when these important issues were settled could Jesus begin His ministry, a ministry that would bring the things of Heaven down to men. The prophecies of Isaiah would suddenly come to life. The lame would walk, the blind would see, the deaf would hear, the dead would return to life, every captive would be set free, and the Light of the world would dispel the darkness so long suffered by man because of the opposing kingdom of Satan. No wonder Satan fought so furiously in this battle! This contest would determine who wore the crown.

The main character in this drama, Jesus, was from the Galilee. When the battle had ended, He, the Victor, came forth out of the wilderness, leaving a defeated foe. Now places of great darkness would see *His Wonders in the Deep.*

CHAPTER 3

THEY "HAVE SEEN A GREAT LIGHT"

*The people who walked in darkness HAVE
SEEN A GREAT LIGHT; those who dwelt in the
land of intense darkness and the shadow of
death, upon them has the Light shined.*

Isaiah 9:2

*Now when Jesus heard that John had been
arrested and put in prison, He withdrew into
Galilee. And leaving Nazareth, He went and
dwelt in Capernaum by the sea, in the country of Zebulun and Naphtali — that what
was spoken by the prophet Isaiah might be
brought to pass: The land of Zebulun and*

Naphtali, in the way to the sea, beyond the Jordan, Galilee of the Gentiles [of the peoples who are not of Israel] — the people who sat (dwelt enveloped) in darkness have seen a great Light, and for those who sat in the land and shadow of death Light has dawned. From that time Jesus began to preach, crying out, Repent (change your mind for the better, heartily amend your ways, with abhorrence of your past sins), for the kingdom of heaven is at hand.

Matthew 4:12-17

What happened at the very beginning of Jesus' ministry is noteworthy. When He heard one day that His cousin, the very same one who had prepared the way for Him with the people of Israel, was now in prison, He decided to move to Galilee.

THE MOVE TO GALILEE

In the natural, Galilee would not have been a logical choice for a good location for a king or for any religious leader of the day. The area was not known for being especially religious. It had not yet become a gathering place for Rabbis, Jewish theologians and Jewish spiritual leaders and teachers. This was not a spiritual hub; it was an agrarian area, a place for farmers and

2

fishermen, many of them im-
migrants from other lands.

Galilee was, in fact, held
in great contempt by the
religious leaders of the day.
As noted in the Amplified
Version of the Bible, it was
known to them as *"Galilee
of the Gentiles."* It was also
known as "Galilee of the
Nations." In fact, *Strong's*
defines the name *Galilee* as
meaning *"heathen circle"*
(*Strong's* #1056).

THE GALILEE OF JESUS' TIME

It was not that the Galilee
was sparsely settled. To the
contrary; according to the
historian Josephus, there
were some two hundred and
forty towns and villages surrounding the Sea of Galilee,
and some of them contained
as many as fifteen thousand
inhabitants. The residents
of these towns were not well
educated people, and their
language skills were often

In the natural, Galilee would not have been a logical choice for a good location for a king or for any religious leader of the day!

subjected to ridicule. The Galileans were not just known as Galileans; they were known as "those Galilean fools."

There was a reason the Galilee was agrarian. Land there was rich and fertile. Corn grew there in abundance, the olive tree flourished, and the fruits and the oil produced from the land were said to be perfect.

The cost of living in the Galilee was only a fifth of that in Judea, and this contributed to the fact that it was a heavily populated area. Most of the inhabitants there were not Jews at all; they were Gentiles. But soon this "Galilee of the Gentiles" would become known as the "Galilee of Jesus." He would become so closely associated with the Galilee that He would sometimes be called "Jesus of Galilee."

What Drew the Savior of the World to This Place?

What was it that drew the Savior of the World and the greatest rabbinical teacher ever (for He was called by many *Rabboni*, teacher) to this place? What compelled Him to direct a great part of His earthly ministry toward the hated populace of the Galilee? According to most, Galilee was a place of great darkness. Even the place known as *"The Valley of the Shadow of Death"* was located close to its boundaries. But Jesus was the Light of the World, and His light could surely dispel (drive away, or disperse) the darkness of that place: *"The people who sat [dwelt enveloped] in darkness have seen a great Light"* (Matthew 4:16). It was there, in the midst of this severe *"darkness"* that Jesus would begin His ministry, and because of this, those who sat in darkness would see *"a great light."*

A Place of Miracles

Jesus would not only base His ministry in the Galilee and on the shores of the Sea of Galilee, but there He would also find His disciples (who would, soon enough, become the great apostles). There, on the Galilee, Jesus would still the storm, and there He would walk on the water.

Many thousands of people would come from every corner of the nation to the Galilee to sit at His feet. There, in that despised and scorned corner of the earth, they would be present when He broke the bread and fed the multitudes. There they would observe the miraculous multiplication of the loaves and fishes and would eat of them. Thus, the hated Galilee, through Jesus of the Galilee and the disciples of the Galilee, would begin to bless the whole earth and to dispel darkness in many places.

It was on the shores of the Galilee that Jesus would deliver the demoniac and turn him into the first Gentile evangelist. There Jesus would heal all manner of sickness and disease. Eventually, His ministry would reach out to many parts of the land and into many of its synagogues, marketplaces, and homes, but it all had its roots in the Galilee, in this place of deep darkness.

Turned Around in the Galilee

It was also there, in the Galilee, that Jesus turned my own life and ministry around, sending me into deeper waters and also into a richer ministry to those who sit in darkness awaiting *"great light."* The once despised Galilee played a great role in my discovery of *His Wonders in the Deep.*

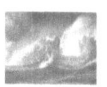

CHAPTER 4

"ROARING DEEP CALLS TO ROARING DEEP"

[Roaring] deep calls to [roaring] deep at the thunder of Your waterspouts; all Your breakers and Your rolling waves have gone over me. Psalm 42:7

The search for the deeper places of God is not a New Testament phenomenon. Old Testament saints also sought it. In Psalm 42, for instance, the psalmist David was longing for the presence of the Lord, and he compared his longing to *"a hart pant[ing] ... for the water brooks"*:

As the hart pants and longs for the water brooks, so I pant and long for You, O God. Psalm 42:1

1

> David was reminded of happier times, when he had led the nation in a mighty procession to the House of God!

DAVID'S THIRST FOR GOD

David's inner man was *"thirst[ing] for ... the living God,"* and he wanted only to see *"the face of God"*:

My inner self thirsts for God, for the living God. When shall I come and behold the face of God?   Psalm 42:2

Tears had been flooding his being so consistently (*"day and night"*) that he called them his *"food"*:

My tears have been my food day and night, while men say to me all day long, Where is your God?   Psalm 42:3

REMEMBERING HAPPIER TIMES

David was reminded of happier times, when he had led the nation in a mighty procession to the House of God. On that day, he had been *"like a bandmaster"* leading a great band, keeping all the members in step with the music:

These things I [earnestly] remember and pour myself out within me: how I went slowly before the throng and led them in procession to the house of God [like a bandmaster before his band, timing the steps to the sound of music and the chant of song] with the voice of shouting and praise, a throng keeping festival.   Psalm 42:4

It occurred to David that this part of his past had been so much grander than his present. He remembered the moment well and knew that in that instant he had been saturated with a sense of fulfillment in who he was. But what was happening to him now? Where was his God?

In those moments of discouragement and depression, David began to ask himself some important questions and, in this way, to examine his *"inner self* (or *soul,* as the King James Version puts it):

Why are you cast down, O my inner self? And why should you moan over me and be disquieted within me?   Psalm 42:5

Suddenly David Knew What He Must Do

Then suddenly, David knew what he must do. "Be quiet!" he said to his soul (his mind,

3

will and emotions). "Here's what you must do":

> *Hope in God and wait expectantly for Him,*
> *for I shall yet praise Him, my Help and my*
> *God.* Psalm 42:5

David forced himself to be calm and to trust God, and suddenly a great change came over him. He had determined that he would not stop praising *"Him"* who was his *"Help"* and his *"God"* — regardless of his current circumstances.

His *"life"* was *"cast down"* at the moment, and he found the *"burden"* of it to be more than he could bear. Still, he was determined to focus on God, his hope and his help:

> *O my God, my life is cast down upon me*
> *[and I find the burden more than I can bear];*
> *therefore I will [earnestly] remember You*
> *from the land of the Jordan [River] and the*
> *[summits of Mount] Hermon, for the little*
> *mountain Mizar.* Psalm 42:6

A Revelation of the Deep

With that, a great transformation began to take place in David's spirit. He had begun to receive a wonderful revelation, a revelation of the deep. It was then that he said:

4

Deep calleth unto deep at the noise of thy waterspouts: all thy waves and thy billows are gone over me.

Psalm 42:7, KJV

Many times I have heard this passage interpreted as meaning that the deep things of God are calling unto the deep things in us, but I'm convinced that this is not the totality of what it means. According to *Strong's*, this first word *deep* refers to "a bottomless pit, the abyss, Hell itself, in which everything is loss." The second *deep* refers to "the profound, the mysteries of God." I see this passage as saying that the lost of this world, those who are dying and going to Hell, are crying out for the deep things of God to come and rescue them. This, then, is our call. As we have seen, this was Jesus' ministry, and He has entrusted it to us. Therefore this is our divine destiny — to

David's "life" was "cast down" at the moment, and he found the "burden" of it to be more than he could bear!

5

first know the deep things of God and then to impart them to others who wait in darkness.

Multitudes Don't Yet Know Christ

The deep is the ocean of humanity, and it is the sea of humanity all around us that is crying out for God's people to come and rescue them. Even though they don't know Him, they're calling out for God. He is still intangible to them, and many of them don't even know who He is.

Multitudes don't yet know the Christ, the Anointed One, who breaks every yoke. Still, all around us a sea of humanity is crying out to God that He might come and rescue them from the abyss, or the deep. Each of us who knows Christ has been rescued from the abyss, often from some very deep pits, our personal Hell on earth. And we were rescued so that we could be sent back to the deep, to the sea of humanity crying out for a God it has never met.

This world is a perilous place filled with incest, molestation, abortion, and the many other curses that are upon its peoples and its nations. I'm sure you know of someone who is right now in a perilous situation. They're all around us. Many times it's nearly impossible to see how such individuals can be rescued out of their private Hell. Unless the God of the Universe comes and delivers them, their pit will only get deeper and darker.

But this is the very reason God wants to send us, to launch us forth into the deep. In launching us into the deep, He is sending us after the sea of humanity locked in the abyss. He is sending us to rescue those who are smothered by incest, those who are dying from molestation, those who still bear the guilt of abortions, those who even now have a murdering spirit raging within them. They are bound by the kingdom of darkness, but we have light to offer them.

Yes, mankind floats in a pit of unmentionable situations, but that's exactly why God wants to launch us forth into the deep — to rescue them.

The Deep Is Mysterious

The deep is mysterious, and there are many mysteries (hidden and obscure things) to be experienced there. Something mysterious is simply something that we have not yet experienced, and, as we noted early on, there are many such things in the deep. Once we have experienced them, they will no longer remain mysterious to us. Jesus has many delicacies prepared for us that we have not yet tasted or enjoyed. Our God has promised:

And I will give you the treasures of darkness and hidden riches of secret places, that you may know that it is I, the Lord, the God of Israel, Who calls you by your name.

Isaiah 45:3

Mysteries are deep things to us, but they're not deep to God, and they're not mysterious to Him. He understands them, and He can reveal them to us. We just need to get into some deeper waters. If we can expect deep things in deep water, it follows that we can expect nothing but shallow things in shallow water.

David's revelation of the deep gave him a glimpse of the sufferings of the sea of humanity he served as king. This caused him to do everything possible to extend the Kingdom of God in the earth, destroy the enemies of God, and bring victory to His people.

What about you? It's time for you to get launched today so that you can experience *His Wonders in the Deep.*

CHAPTER 5

"LAUNCH OUT INTO THE DEEP"

Now it occurred while the people pressed upon Jesus to hear the message of God, he was standing by the lake of Gennesaret (Sea of Galilee) ...   Luke 5:1

Having been to Israel now several times, when I read this, I get a wonderful and meaningful visual image of just where this story took place. We cannot know for sure in just which spot around the lake it happened. Since the Galilee is quite large, it could have happened at any number of places — perhaps in Capernaum or Tiberias. Who can say for sure?

Wherever it happened, many people, probably thousands of them, were so anxious to hear Jesus' words that they *pressed upon [Him]."* Looking for a way to accommodate them all, Jesus decided to get into one of the many boats that were used around the lake for fishing and transportation and to preach from that vantage point:

> *And He saw two boats drawn up by the lake, but the fisherman had gone down from them and were washing their nets. And getting into one of the boats, [the one] that belonged to Simon (Peter), He requested him to draw away a little from the shore. Then He sat down and continued to teach the crowd [of people] from the boat.* Luke 5:2-3

The disciples may not have known it at the time, but they were about to be launched out into the deep. And you and I, too, are about to be launched out. Some will be launched in greater measure than others, but all of us will be sent forth into the deeper things of God — if we are willing.

The Crowds Made It Necessary

The crowds of people who were standing near the shore made it necessary for Jesus to get out into deeper water before He could minister to them. The multitudes and their needs pressed against Him, forcing Him to minister in deeper waters. Too often, we insist on staying in the shallow places. We've had some wonderful experiences with God, but we feel comfortable staying in the most shallow part of those experiences. Now it's time to launch out into deeper places.

When Jesus had finished speaking that day, He had something else in mind for His disciples:

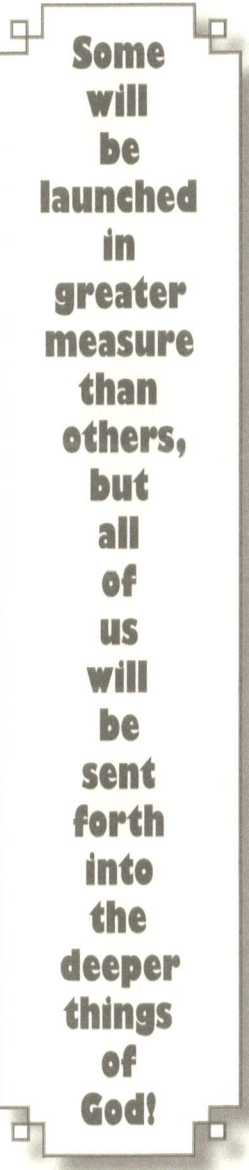

Some will be launched in greater measure than others, but all of us will be sent forth into the deeper things of God!

> *When He had stopped speaking, He said to Simon (Peter), Put out into the deep [water] {LAUNCH OUT INTO THE DEEP, KJV], and lower your nets for a haul.* Luke 5:4

We all know the story. Peter argued that he had already tried, but nothing had happened. We can all understand this reaction. We've had the very same experience ourselves. But Jesus knew

3

that the time was now right, and He commanded Peter to go into deeper water and let his nets
down again.

This is a wonderful secret for harvesting. If
we can get launched out into deeper waters,
we'll take in more fish. We've been in shallow
waters too long, and God's desire is to launch
us into the deep.

Each of us has a great destiny, but if we just
stand on the shoreline and listen, we'll never
accomplish great things for God's Kingdom. It's
time to launch out into the deep so that we can
bring in a greater harvest.

Deepness Is Relative

Shallowness and deepness are, of course,
relative. Some water may seem deep to you, but
once you see the depth of what God really wants
to do in your life, suddenly you'll realize that the
water you've been standing in has been terribly
shallow.

You may have tried harvesting for the Lord,
and the catch was not what it should have
been. But when we launch into the deep at His
command and in His timing, there is always a
multitude of fish to be caught.

Peter and the others had *"toiled all night [ex-
haustingly]"* and still they had *"caught nothing"*
(Luke 5:5). That's no fun, but the key is to do

4

things in God's time and in His way. He knows when the time is just right for any endeavor. He knows when the windows of Heaven are open. When He speaks, go ahead and cast your nets into the deep, and it will work — even when exactly the same thing has not worked before.

It would have done Peter no good to lower his nets right where he was. The water was too shallow there. He first had to launch out into the deep before anything of consequence could happen.

The Needed Depths

Simon Peter's answer to Jesus reflected his impatience with his fishing. He had fished unsuccessfully the whole night, and he was more than ready to call it quits. Many times we must be faithful for an entire season before we see the increase God has promised us. If we trust Him and believe what He says, the harvest will come (in its appointed time).

Peter deeply respected His Lord. So, even though he had reason to object to what Jesus was saying, he went on to say:

But on the ground of Your word, I will lower the nets [again]. Luke 5:5

The King James Version of the Bible says it this way:

Nevertheless at thy word I will let down the net.   Luke 5:5, KJV

Peter believed that Jesus always told the truth, and he was willing to act on the basis of His word — even if he didn't understand it. Thank God we don't have to move on the basis of our own words, but we can act on His word. Because He said it, we can move on it. Because He spoke it, we can act and expect results. And when we launch into the deep, at His command and by faith in His words, God is always faithful to reward us.

Simon Peter had to do something! He had to act!

In the natural, Peter saw no reason to act, but he knew Jesus, and he knew that he could trust what Jesus said. Therefore he acted — even though his instincts told him to do otherwise. So Peter launched into the deep.

Action Is Required

This word *launch*, according to *Young's*, means "put out." In other words, Simon Peter had to do something. He had to act. He had been cleaning his nets, getting ready to put them up for the day, but now Jesus told him to get ready to set them out again. He had worked all night *"exhaustingly,"* and he was tired, and what Jesus was saying didn't seem to make much sense. Still, because Jesus had said it, Peter obeyed and did it, and the result was wonderful:

> And when they had done this, they caught a great number of fish; and ... their nets were [at the point of] breaking.   Luke 5:6

When the disciples of Jesus became willing to launch out into deeper water and to let down their nets again (despite the failures of the past), there was such a great harvest that the very nets they had thrown out during the night season and caught nothing were now suddenly filled. It was such a *"draught of fish,"* that they could hardly pull the nets back in.

Had the times changed that much? Not really. Had the water shifted? Was there a cool breeze that somehow made that much difference? Had the water itself warmed or cooled? Did a great school of fish just happen to come swimming by at that particular moment? Of course not. Nothing had changed ... except that it was now the right moment, and the disciples were acting in obedience to God in deeper waters. If, then, I am obedient and do what God bids me, I can expect a harvest too. I can expect to receive what I haven't been able to obtain for myself through long and arduous toil.

Sometimes we have been waiting for a long while, and nothing seems to be happening. Then, suddenly, everything is happening at once, and it's because the timing is right, and we become willing to launch out into deeper waters. In these moments, there comes to us such a great abundance that we cannot carry it all, and we're forced to be generous with others.

Launching Demands a Freedom on Your Part

This word *launch*, according to *Strong's*, also means "to thrust out," This implies a freedom on your part to act. When you are able to launch into the deep, many times it will be because you have been freed to do so. It happens because someone else, our Redeemer, has broken through every existing impediment for you. Such breakthroughs come when one moment you're on one side of a situation, and the next moment you find yourself on the other side of it. Something or Someone has thrust you right through every circumstance, and you can now be obedient to God and go forth to bring in the waiting harvest. But you cannot launch into the deep if you're not free to do so.

A Departure Is in Store

Launch also means "to sail away, to set forth, to put out to sea, to loose or be released, to sail on." When there's a launching, it denotes a departure. Your ship is being loosed from its moorings, and you will soon set sail for some deeper waters. Most of us have been wading around in shallow water far too long. We have wanted to behave ourselves and not act too bold or too strong, but God is saying, "Launch out! Take the plunge!" So, go ahead. Be bold! It's your time for harvest!

You may suddenly begin to prophesy, to sing a new song or to teach or preach. Just get yourself launched. Let God release you and then put you out to sea. When He sets your sail, the results will always be wonderful!

Sail away, set forth, put out to sea, get loose, sail on ... these are all action words, commands, imperatives, so they require some action on our part. Launching into the deep requires steps of faith, but your reward will be a new profundity, a new depth in your spirit and in your everyday life. And one thing is certain: you will never experience anything profound in shallow waters, so move on out.

A Miraculous Draught

Again, as Simon Peter now lowered his nets, he probably did it in exactly the way he had always done it before. There was nothing new in his technique. Still, this time, it worked, and it was only because it had been done in the Lord's timing, at the Lord's command, and at a greater depth.

The miraculous draught of fishes had nothing to do with who Simon Peter was or what ability he possessed. It didn't have anything to do with the wind or the weather. It was all because of three elements: God's timing, God's commissioning and the depth of the water being fished.

When God's timing becomes apparent to you, because He speaks for you to act, and you launch out into the deep, you may do the same thing you did yesterday and do it in the very same way, but the result this time will be different. That result may be so wonderful that you will barely be able to contain it. God is no respecter of persons. What He did for Peter He will do for you too.

The Dangerous Element of Launching

There is also a dangerous, or scary, element to launching into greater depths or launching forth at all. After all, you're leaving the known and moving into the unknown, and you're leaving the secure and trusting God to keep you in the deep.

This dangerous element to the launch might frighten some or cause some to be hesitant. Stepping into the unknown brings this element of hesitation. Since I have experienced so much of the miraculous, it gives me a sense of living on the edge and believing the Lord for the impossible. This is called faith, and with faith as my partner, because I want what's out there in the deep, I'm willing to take the accompanying risks to see God move.

In this same vein, to *launch* can mean "to begin something large, a hazardous undertaking." On the one hand, it might speak of something grand, but it can also denote something scary, even hazardous to your health. Are you ready to trust God to keep you through whatever might come? The unknown might frighten you sometimes, but believe me, you'll enjoy the ride, and you can trust God to keep you every step of the way.

> **Are you ready to trust God to keep you through whatever might come?**

Moving into the Deeper Places Prepared for Us

Think about it: Peter was one of the Lord's chosen disciples, and yet he had been in shallow water, and it was time for him to launch out into the deep. Even when we have already done great and mighty things in the Kingdom of God, we may find ourselves in shallow waters ... in comparison to what God's desire for our lives is or in comparison to what He has for us just on the horizon.

Peter surely must have been thinking, "Lord, I'm doing the best I know how." After all, he was an experienced fisherman, so he knew where to fish and when. As we already noted, he objected to the idea of letting down the nets again, but Jesus insisted that he try one more time, this time in deeper water, and, thank God, Peter obeyed.

When Jesus said to Peter, *"Launch out into the deep,"* He meant that Peter was being sent forth from his current position and being moved on out to the deeper places the Lord had prepared for him. This spoke to Peter's heart, he responded favorably, and the harvest he reaped as a result was notable.

How God Speaks Today

When God spoke to Peter that day, Jesus was there in the flesh to do it, but God continues to speak to us in many ways today. He speaks through His Word and through prophetic utterance, and He speaks through dreams and visions, but He can also speak to us through the daily news or through a television program. It's happened to me many times. I can't tell you how very many times I have turned on the television just to lie for a few moments in our chaise lounge and relax, and the Spirit of the Lord was right there, speaking to me prophetically through what I was seeing and hearing.

One day I was working in the yard, something I don't get to do nearly often enough, and my daughter Elizabeth, still a teenager at the time, came running out to tell me that she had just heard a line in an old movie, just as I had preached it recently from God's Word. It is wonderful the way God confirms our destinies to us through everyday life. Allow Him to speak to you in His own way, and He will surely send you forth into deeper places.

Get Ready to Sail Away

Again, this phrase *launch out,* which Jesus spoke to Peter, can mean "to sail away, to depart, to go out, to sail on." Some of you will soon set sail for faraway places. God wants to launch some of us into the marketplace, into the business world, and into the academic world, but others are destined to be launched into all sorts of ministries. God's Kingdom is exploding in the earth, and He is allowing those who will to play their part in that expansion.

In certain seasons of our lives, we just seem to sail around in our common experience, but we are now in a new season, and it's time to sail on into the deeper places God has prepared for us. The wonderful thing to know is that, whatever else this may mean, it means bigger catches in the future.

Deeper Water Accommodates Bigger Fish

As we noted, part of Peter's failure to catch fish, after toiling all night, was that he had not been in deep enough waters. That's because fish don't usually stay in shallow waters. They much prefer the deep.

Close to the shore, where the water is shallow, only minnows can be seen, and minnows don't make very good food. They're much too

> It is also in the deep that your greatest fruitfulness, your greatest spiritual catches will take place!

tiny. But the deeper you go, the larger the fish you'll find. And the deeper you go in God, the more anointing you'll find, the more signs and wonders you'll experience, and the bigger the fish you'll catch.

It's hard to operate in shallow waters, so when God launches you into the deep, He also expands your boundaries. Your ministry will increase in depth in accordance with the depth of the spiritual waters you're swimming in. Why stay so confined? Why limit your influence?

It is also in the deep that your greatest fruitfulness, your greatest spiritual catches will take place. So what are you waiting for? Launch out into the deep today.

Each of us is called to reach people for God, so the choice is ours. We can concentrate on a few minnows in the shallow places, or we can launch out into the deep and reach multitudes.

Use Your Nets Well

The men of Peter's day used very large nets with weights on the bottom of them and some sort of object that floated that held them upright in the water. When the nets were thrown out, they sometimes covered a large area. As they were pulled in, the floats kept the top of the net stable while the weights caused the lower portion to drag against the bottom. This trapped the fish inside, and as the nets were drawn in, the fish had nowhere to escape. Your nets will be just as effective if you can get launched into some deeper waters. So what are you waiting for? Launch out into the deep. God wants to give you rivers to swim in, rivers of anointing, rivers of glory, more people to touch, bigger fish to catch. Hear His voice today and respond positively.

What God has for you tomorrow, next week, next month, and next year will cause you to become more effective in the Kingdom. We're operating in the Kingdom already, but when you're called into deeper waters, it's because God has a plan for you to become more effective and more fruitful in His Kingdom. Get ready. You're about to behold *His Wonders in the Deep.*

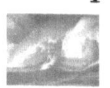

CHAPTER 6

PREPARING TO BE LAUNCHED

This word *launch* that we are considering has another meaning. It is not just something *you* do; it can also be something that is done *to* you. In this sense, it means to be thrust out or thrust forth.

YOU NEED TO BE LAUNCHED

In this sense, launch means "the act of causing something to be propelled upward or forward," "the act of propelling a rocket into space," "to send forth, as in the launch of a rocket," "the act of causing a glider to become airborne," "to cause a plan to become active."

You need to be launched. If you were meant to soar, you won't be happy until you do. Eagles don't do well in chicken coops. They cannot remain earthbound; they have to soar. They love the feel of the wind under their wings, lifting them higher.

Most of us have a lot of plans that have never become operative. It's time that our plans get launched. You and your dreams for the future are about to be launched into some deeper waters where you can safely and fruitfully operate.

> Only He can do the actual launching! We are powerless to launch ourselves!

An Important Distinction

There is an important distinction in this meaning of *launch* compared to the *launch* we considered in the last chapter. When we launch into the deep, there is an action required on our part. We put out to sea, we go out, we sail on, we set forth. In the case of a rocket, however, it cannot possibly launch itself; it must be launched. In the same way, there are things that we can do to get ready to be launched into ministry or into new favor with God, but only He can do the actual launching. We are powerless to launch ourselves.

This is seen clearly in another meaning of the word *launch*. It also means "the act of commissioning a newly-built ship, by moving it from the land into the water." Such a launch is important because ships are not made for land; they're made for the water. A ship may be built on land, but it's not made to stay on land. It's made to sail the deep, and on land it serves little purpose.

The same is true of you. You have been created to sail the deep, and your full fruitfulness will come only when you've had the Lord break the bonds that hold you, so that you are then free to sail forth. You, like a great ship and its captain, may be ready to begin a journey in your intended purpose, but before this can happen, you, just like the ship, must be launched.

What does it mean to be launched? It means "to be thrust out." Some of you are even now on the launching pad, and the final adjustments are being made to your life so that you can be launched. You're not quite ready, but almost. Your launch is coming. At the right season, in God's perfect time, He will place you on His launchpad and send you forth into greater fruitfulness.

Because of the much publicized launches of the Space Shuttle, we all learned something about what it takes to launch such a craft. We're now familiar with what is commonly called "the launch-pad," and we have all heard much about the acceptable "launch window." These are important elements for us in the Spirit world as well.

THE LAUNCHPAD

With the Space Shuttle program (and its related rocket firings), the launchpad was a platform from which the rocket was launched. Years were spent creating these magnificent ships that could orbit in space, but if there was not some sort of launchpad, and the ship was never actually placed on that launchpad and then launched into space, it would have remained little more than an expensive ornament, an extravagant curiosity.

Each shuttle was a work of art. Just completing the miles of wiring required to operate all of its sophisticated equipment was a feat to be admired. And there were many other systems in each shuttle that were just as complicated, just as demanding, and just as critical. When one of those ships was launched into orbit, there could be no short-circuited breakers or other failing systems. Everything had to be fully operational because there was so much at stake. Therefore,

4

preparations were extensive, and nothing could be overlooked.

Those craft did very little good sitting in a hanger at Cape Canaveral. When everything was in readiness, the ship had to be moved to the launchpad and prepared for launch. Everything else had been preparation for that critical moment.

GET YOURSELF INTO PLACE

With the Space Shuttle, if the ship had not reached the launchpad by the indicated launch time, there could be no launch. It was as simple as that. When the shuttle was late in arriving (for any reason), the projected launch was canceled, and a new launch date had to be contemplated.

If you want to be shot out into spiritual space, if you want to be launched forth for God, you have to get yourself into place. Get onto God's launch platform, and be there at the right moment, in God's perfect timing. It's not enough to be sitting in some warehouse saying, "I'm ready," and yet this, I'm afraid, is exactly what many do. You may have all the wires connected and have all the other necessary parts in place. Everything may be ready, but without the launch, nothing worthwhile will happen, and all the preparation will be in vain.

In a spiritual sense, this could be compared with having faith to believe that God will use you and yet lacking the discipline to get yourself into place so that He can start doing it. You can't just sit back doing nothing and expect God to launch you forth. You have to get moving. You have to do something to get yourself onto the launchpad.

Your Particular Launchpad

Your launchpad, or launch platform, may be different from mine, but whatever it is, you have to be on it. If God has called you to do something, you have to be there, ready for Him to manifest His power through your life when the time comes. Get yourself onto the launchpad and be there on time, and you will find that God never fails to do His part.

A launchpad is a springboard. In a spiritual sense, it may be some position in a local church ministry, so your launchpad may be a church platform. But in a very real sense, your personal relationship with Christ Jesus is your platform. Anything that you accomplish in life will come out of that experience. Get onto the platform and get ready.

The Most Critical Part

The process of launching rockets was one of the most critical and difficult parts of the entire Space Program. Many things could go wrong and did go wrong during the launch, so it was always a rather scary and tense period. Once a rocket was actually in the air, we all breathed a sigh of relief. Until that moment, we couldn't be sure if things would go right or not.

Aside from the detailed preparations that went on behind the scenes, there were several critical elements of the launch to consider:

THE COUNTDOWN:

The moments of countdown, as the great ship prepared for takeoff, were always very tense for the astronauts and also for the space engineers controlling the flight. Some astronauts had died on the launchpad because something didn't go right, something was not in its place, something did not function as planned. These were critical moments, and everything had to be right.

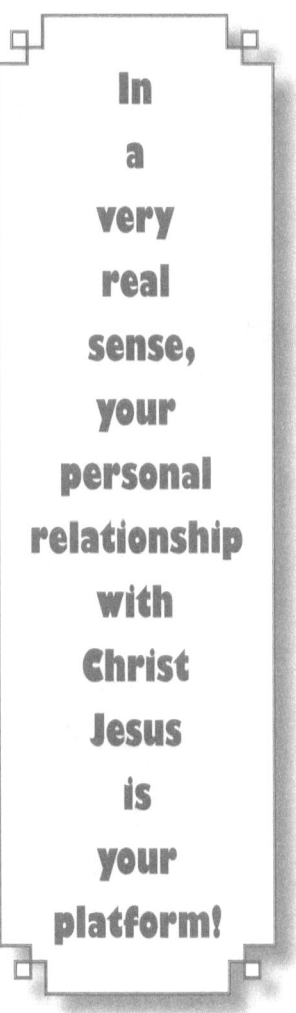

In a very real sense, your personal relationship with Christ Jesus is your platform!

THE LAUNCH WINDOW:

There was also what scientists came to call the launch window. This was a period of time in which all existing conditions on the earth at the launch site and in the air above it were considered to be optimal. The weather was a vital factor in considering the proper launch window, especially the temperature and the wind direction and speed. There had to be an absence of major storms in the area, for the launch required a certain calmness. And, because so much had been invested in the preparations of a rocket, it could not be launched until every condition was perfect or, at the very least, in the range of acceptability.

A launch window was very critical to any mission's success, and the conditions had to be just right because so much was at stake. Billions of dollars had been invested in these launches, and so no chances could be taken.

In the same way, none of us wants to be launched under anything other than perfect conditions. So much is at stake that we don't want to take chances with our launch. It has to be right.

The most serious spiritual launches involve profound leaps into the unknown. Some are willing just to take whatever comes, but others of us long to be launched into the very important places in the Spirit. Get ready to be launched, for God is even now defining your launch window.

8

The proper launch window for any given space flight was determined by those who studied the weather and the positioning of the heavenly bodies that might, in any way, affect the mission. Spiritually, our launch window can be determined only by God Himself. Only He knows about every condition that might affect us, and therefore only He can make a judgment about when the timing is right for us to be launched. Far too many have been launched when *they* considered the time to be right, only to have a failed mission, a crash landing, or worse — a personal tragedy.

Your launch window is not like that of any other living person. Each of us is different, and our circumstances are different. A decision on the proper timing for launch, therefore, is so complex that it would be utterly foolish for any of us to try to make it. Only God knows the details of all that He has called you to do. Only He knows what has been planned for your life. We often seem to stumble onto it, and we're almost always surprised. We were not expecting it, but He has known the timing of it all along and was guiding the process toward that end.

A Window of Opportunity:

We sometimes call a launch window a "window of opportunity." This means that everything has lined up perfectly. You've gotten yourself onto the launchpad, and you're there waiting. Periodically, you may feel that the time is right for launch, and you may say to the Lord, "Okay, God! I'm ready to be launched." But only He truly knows the precise moment to actually do it. So trust Him implicitly.

You may get restless and wonder why those in control are not initiating the launch, but the truth is that this launch is under the control of the Spirit of God. Rest in this knowledge, for He always knows best. Men may seem to be in control of your life, but in reality, they cannot be. Only God can do that. When His time is right, you will be launched.

You may have been waiting a long time, and your night season may have seemed interminably long. It may actually seem that nothing is happening in your life or ministry, that you're making no progress whatsoever at getting to where you want to go. You may have been doing all the right things and saying the right things, and still it seems that nothing is happening. When this is true, sometimes the tick of the clock may seem endless.

But then, just when you thought all hope was lost, another tick is heard, and the engines suddenly explode into life. The much-anticipated launch window has finally arrived. The moment is right. All obstacles have been removed, and you feel the vibrations of the ship as it prepares for blastoff.

Oh, beloved, it's time. God is about ready to deliver you. He is about to give you your breakthrough.

Some of you are still in the shop being built. Some are in a storage shed, waiting to be summoned. Others of you are on the launchpad, just waiting for the ideal launch window to open.

Interestingly enough, the Hebrew word for launch is *nasa,* matching the acronym for our National Aeronautics and Space Administration (NASA). Was that just a coincidence or what?

Get ready. Your launch date is coming. Then, you will surely see *His Wonders in the Deep.*

CHAPTER 7

COMPELLED TO GO

Then Paul replied, What do you mean by weeping and breaking my heart like this? For I hold myself in readiness not only to be arrested and bound and imprisoned at Jerusalem, but also [even] to die for the name of the Lord Jesus. Acts 21:13

The apostle Paul, too, was launched. At one critical point in his life, he felt compelled to go to Jerusalem, even though he was repeatedly warned along the way that such a visit would be dangerous for him.

The Warnings

The respected prophet Agabus approached Paul one day and began to bind his sash around the apostle and to say that this is what would happen to him if he insisted on going to Jerusalem. Paul's reply was that he had no control over the circumstance. He was ready for whatever lay ahead, but he simply had to get to Jerusalem.

This determination was not made, as some have suggested, because Paul was being disobedient or rebellious. Rather, it was because he was a bond slave to Jesus, and it didn't matter to him what price he had to pay to fulfill God's call upon his life. He must get to Jerusalem, regardless of the cost. He was being pulled into the deep, compelled to go despite all the well-meaning warnings.

What Was Paul Feeling?

Paul was being launched into the unknown, and we can only imagine how he was feeling about that fact. Sensing that he probably would not come back this way for quite some time, if ever, he called for the elders from Ephesus and, when they had come to him, he admonished them in a lengthy message. Part of what he said to those men that day was recorded for us by Luke in the book of Acts. Toward the end of that admonition, Paul spoke these words:

Therefore be always alert and on your guard, being mindful that for three years I never stopped night or day seriously to admonish and advise and exhort you one by one with tears. And now [brethren], I commit you to God [I deposit you in His charge, entrusting you to His protection and care]. And I commend you to the Word of His grace [to the command and counsels and promises of His unmerited favor]. It is able to build you up and to give you [your rightful] inheritance among all God's set-apart ones (those consecrated, purified, and transformed of soul). I coveted no man's silver, or gold, or [costly] garments. You yourselves know personally that these hands ministered to my own needs and those [of the persons] who were with me.

Acts 20:31-34

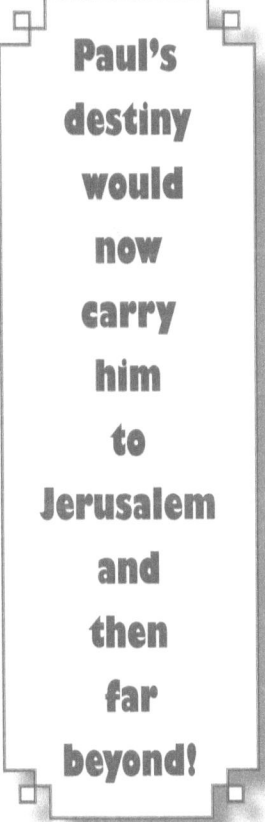

Paul's destiny would now carry him to Jerusalem and then far beyond!

When Paul exhorted the people with many "tears," it was because he sensed that he would never see them again. His destiny would now carry him to Jerusalem and then far beyond. All that he had done for them he had done out of a pure heart. He had not coveted *"{any} man's silver, or gold, or [costly] garments."* He had, in fact, made tents to support himself, so that he would not be financially beholden to any man.

An Astonishing Response

Some of the things Paul said that day made these followers know that he was ready even to die for his faith, and the response this provoked is moving:

> *Having spoken thus, he knelt down with them all and prayed. And they all wept freely and threw their arms around Paul's neck and kissed him fervently and repeatedly, being especially distressed and sorrowful because he had stated that they were about to see his face no more. And they accompanied him to the ship.* Acts 20:36-38

Paul was about to be launched into a new and mysterious adventure, and his followers were also about to be launched into a deeper ministry of their own. Along his journey to Jerusalem, Paul would meet many comrades, many young disciples and apostles-to-be, and among them would be Philip, the great evangelist. Philip and many of the other people Paul met on this trip were about to be launched into something new and wonderful, and Paul was determined to be part of their destiny — no matter what it cost him.

DEEPLY MOVED

The elders of the church at Ephesus were among those who received Paul's vision and mantle in those days. That they were deeply moved is apparent from Luke's account. Paul and his other traveling companions had to tear themselves away from these Ephesian leaders:

And when we had torn ourselves away from them and withdrawn, we set sail.
                                        Acts 21:1

The King James Version says that they *"launched."* Why? Paul knew that he must fulfill his destiny, even if t meant imprisonment and death. Upon arriving in Jerusalem, he would be imprisoned and would, from then on, enjoy very little freedom ever again. In the end, he would be sent to Rome to stand trial. He was being launched into the unknown.

In a very real sense of the word, the men who accompanied Paul to the ship that day were also being launched. Because Paul was moving on to other things, God wanted to raise

God
is
giving
you
the
right
of
passage
and
is
preparing
many
cities
for
you
to
visit
for
His
glory!

up new apostles and teachers, new spiritual fathers for the flock, so Paul's traveling companions were also being launched into deeper experiences. They had not been required to be there with him, but they chose to be there. They, too, had a destination, a destiny.

Some Chose to Accompany Paul

Some of the men who heard Paul address the Ephesian elders that day chose to accompany him on his journey. Luke, the beloved physician, was one of them, and in his narrative, recording the history of the early church, he named some of the places he, Paul, and the rest of the team would now pass:

We set sail and made a straight run to Cos, and on the following [day came] to Rhodes and from there to Patara. There we found a

ship crossing over to Phoenicia; so we went
aboard and sailed away.   Acts 21:1-2

Again, aside from Paul, those who were represented by Luke's *"we"* did not have to be there.
Paul was being launched, but the others chose
to be launched with him. No one would have
blamed them if they had decided to stay behind,
but they didn't. They accompanied their beloved
brother, first to one place, and then to another.

What took place in each of the various cities
they visited we can only imagine. The Bible is not
large enough to tell it all. We can be sure that
each place they passed held spiritual adventure
for all of them. We do know that in one city they
would meet Philip and his four daughters, who
were prophetesses, and those daughters would
speak forth the word of the Lord to Paul. But
few other details are given. Surely, great signs
and wonders must have followed Paul and his
company everywhere they went.

EVENTUALLY SENT TO ROME

At a later time, Paul was sent to Rome and,
again, he and those who chose to accompany
him were launched forth on a journey into the
unknown. They went from city to city, state to
state, and country to country. They ministered
to others, and they themselves were ministered

to. Get ready for your own journey. God is giving you the right of passage and is preparing many cities for you to visit for His glory.

You may just be a tail feather in God's arrow, or you may be the shaft or the actual arrowhead. But it doesn't matter which. You are being sent forth, so you will have a share of the spoils.

Does this include women? Of course it does! Kathryn Kuhlman did much to prepare the way for us ladies to minister today. Joyce Meyer has been used of God in this regard. Ruth Ward Heflin helped to prepare the way for women in ministry as well. And every great person of faith of recent ages — male and female alike — has had a part. As they faced down the forces of darkness, they left in their wake great spoils of battle that we are even now still gathering in. Their launch made our journey much easier.

We owe a great debt of gratitude to Abraham, Isaac, and Jacob. They made our walk with God so much easier. We, in turn, are preparing the way for those who will come after us.

Because of the sacrifice of others, we have been given the rights of passage, and this has made it possible for us to walk in the deep — whether we understand that yet or not.

"They Launched Forth"

And they launched forth.   Luke 8:22, KJV

Paul and his companions *"launched forth."* At some point, there comes to our lives a sensing, a knowing, that God is about to do something very special for us. He is about to launch us out into deeper places, and now is one of those times.

You are like a ship that is about to be launched. As noted earlier, a ship that stayed on land wouldn't serve a useful purpose. It was not made for land. It was made to launch out into the deep places of the earth, and only when it has been launched can it fulfill its intended purpose.

You're like a glider that is about to be sent aloft. A glider was not meant to remain on the ground, so get ready to fly. Gliders are made to launch into the air.

Again, What Are We without the Launch?

As we noted earlier, the process of building a great ship is impressive, but that process means nothing if the launching never comes. The technology that has permitted us to build ever lighter and more powerful gliders is impressive, but all of the effort is in vain if the glider is never launched.

At some point, we have to be placed on the launching pad, and at some point the right moment has to arrive for being sent forth for our intended purpose. Get ready to launch.

A glider that is kept stored in some hanger may have some value to someone, but it certainly cannot lay claim to success. That glider might look very impressive sitting there in the hanger, but you were not made to be looked upon. Get out on the launching pad, and believe God to send you forth today.

Like Paul, you may have the experience of being compelled to go or to do. Welcome it, for it is in this way that you will come to know *His Wonders in the Deep.*

CHAPTER 8

THRUST FORTH

Then the Lord said to Moses, Yet will I bring one more plague on Pharaoh and on Egypt; afterwards he will let you go. When he lets you go from here, he will thrust you out altogether.

Exodus 11:1

Another meaning for the word *launch* is "thrust out" or "thrust forth," and, again, it is something that is done *to* us, not something that we do for ourselves. We can only get ready and wait for it to happen.

GOD'S CALL UPON MOSES

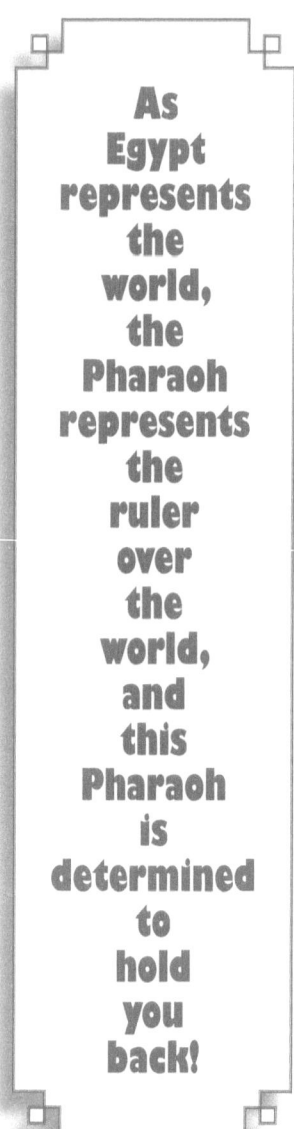

As Egypt represents the world, the Pharaoh represents the ruler over the world, and this Pharaoh is determined to hold you back!

When God called Moses to deliver the children of Israel from bondage in Egypt, Moses was willing, but it was nothing he could do himself. God would have to do it. Then Moses had a visitation from God, and as God directed him, he began to position himself and the people to be thrust out of Pharaoh's grip. In a sense, he got himself and them onto the launchpad and then waited for the proper time to launch.

God said, *"He will thrust you out altogether,"* so you need to get ready, because you are about to be delivered from your pharaohs. As Egypt represents the world, the Pharaoh represents the ruler over the world, and this Pharaoh is determined to hold you back. God says, *"He will let you go."* Very soon now your release will come, and when you are released from bondage, your launching forth is imminent. You will soon be thrust out. Your long-awaited breakthrough is coming.

TAKEN BY SURPRISE

Not only would Pharaoh let Moses go; he would also *"thrust [him] out."* When this happens to you, you may be taken by surprise. You may have been standing by, feeling ready for a while now, but releases come suddenly. Breakthroughs come suddenly. Windows of opportunity come suddenly. Your window of opportunity may soon open over you without warning. Be ready for it when it does come, and don't allow it to pass without launching forth.

There is a right season for everything. Like Esther, you have been born into the Kingdom for *"such a time as this"* (Esther 4:14), but only God can say just when that perfect time is. Stay ready always so that you won't miss your appointed time.

LET GOD DECIDE THE TIMING

When Moses spoke forth the first plague against the Pharaoh and Egypt, as the Lord had commanded, he must have expected that his deliverance would come instantly. When it didn't, and he had to speak another plague and another, it must have been a trying experience for him. Nothing seemed to be working. But the deliverance of the people of Israel was only one plague away. They were about to be thrust out, and Moses only needed to be patient a little while longer.

It's very important that you focus on what God has told you to get ready for and that you make every preparation for it. God never fails to thrust us forth — when we have readied ourselves. God said to Moses:

Speak now in the hearing of the people, and let every man solicit and ask of his neighbor, and every woman of her neighbor, jewels of silver and jewels of gold. Exodus 11:2

This was God's way of saying to the Israelites, "Your window of opportunity is opening." They were about to go out, so they needed to prepare for the journey. They needed to borrow vessels from their Egyptian neighbors. In this way, God had prepared for their provision on the journey. They would go out full, carrying the gold and silver vessels of their former "hosts."

God has many unusual ways of meeting our needs. Sometimes He supplies for us through the grocery store or the shopping mall, but many times He does it in much more unusual ways. You can know that He will never launch you out without providing for your journey.

THE SIGNIFICANCE OF THE PASSOVER MEAL

When God promised to deliver His people from Egypt, He told them He wanted to celebrate a feast with them. This was not unusual because He is always desiring to feast with His people:

> *Afterward Moses and Aaron went in and told Pharaoh, Thus says the Lord, the God of Israel, Let My people go, that they may hold a feast to Me in the wilderness.*
>
> Exodus 5:1

> *And Moses said, We will go with our young and our old, with our sons and our daughters, with our flocks and our herds [all of us and all we have], for we must hold a feast to the Lord.* Exodus 10:9

Before they ever left Egypt, however, they celebrated the first Feast of Passover. They were to celebrate this feast with their shoes on and their walking sticks in their hands. They had to be ready for the journey, for the launch. They had to be ready, for God was about to cause them to be thrust forth, thrust out from their bondage to Pharaoh. This is why the Lord tells us, as believers in Christ:

And having shod your feet in preparation [to face the enemy with the firm-footed stability, the promptness, and the readiness produced by the good news] of the Gospel of peace ...
                                    Ephesians 6:15

The King James Version of the Bible says it this way:

[Having] your feet shod with the preparation of the gospel of peace ...

God was about to thrust the children of Israel out of Egypt, but they had to be ready. So let this be a lesson to us. Get ready. Put your shoes on, have the staff in your hand, and eat your meal in haste.

In the case of the children of Israel in Egypt, their meal was also to be eaten with great anticipation. It was to be the last meal eaten in bondage. The time was at hand for them to be delivered and launched forth, thrust out, and God wanted them to act like they were expecting something better.

Get Ready

Get ready. God is about to open your launch window. Conditions are nearing perfection.

Everything is lining up. I'm ready to go. Are you?

Are your shoes on? Is your staff in your hand? Are you eating with excitement in your soul? Are you ready for your deliverance? Are you ready to be launched into the deep? Are you expecting something better or something greater? I hope so, for the time is fast approaching.

GET INTO PLACE

Again, when the moment comes for the button to be pushed, you must be in place. If not, God can't activate your launch. Just as the conditions must be perfect for a launch to take place at Cape Canaveral, I wouldn't want my King to push the button and launch me out until every condition was right.

Again, you must have a launching pad. God doesn't place inactive people into the ministry. He looks for those

Are your shoes on? Is your staff in your hand? Are you eating with excitement in your soul?

who are busy in some corner of His vineyard, and He increases their anointing to do a new work. Don't wait for your launch before you start doing something. Put your hand to the plow even now, and then refuse to look back.

Get Busy Doing Something for the Kingdom

Not everyone has to be on a public platform. It helps, but some people are busy for God on the telephone, and others are busy for Him in the shopping center. Let the love and compassion of Jesus pour out of you wherever you are. There are, however, some clear principles in God's Word that can help us find a place of launching in the Kingdom:

The Lord God hath given me the tongue of the learned, that I should know how to speak a word in season to him that is weary: he wakeneth morning by morning, he wakeneth mine ear to hear as the learned.
Isaiah 50:4, KJV

Preach the word; be instant in season, out of season; reprove, rebuke, exhort with all long suffering and doctrine.
2 Timothy 4:2, KJV

Study and be eager and do your utmost to present yourself to God approved (tested by trial), a workman who has no cause to be ashamed, correctly analyzing and accurately dividing [rightly handling and skillfully teaching] the Word of Truth.

2 Timothy 2:15

"Speak a word in season," "be instant in season, out of season," "Study ... to present yourself to God approved," ... these are very good places to start. If you're just sitting around doing nothing, you can't expect God to come and zap you one day and launch you forth. He needs to see your hands on the plow.

Elisha Was Found Plowing

When the mantle of Elijah passed to the younger Elisha, he was in the field of Abelmahola, which means "the field of dancers." What does this indicate? It show us that Elisha was a worshiper. He knew how to rejoice in God, as well as how to put his hand to the plow.

In the very moment when Elijah arrived, Elisha was driving a team of twelve oxen (twelve being the number of the apostolic). He was already serving in the Kingdom. So if you want to get launched into deeper things, put your hand to the plow. Get busy in God's vineyard. Do something meaningful for the Kingdom. Then you become a candidate for the launching pad.

The fact that you're even now awaiting launch does not necessarily mean that you've been doing nothing. It simply means that you are moving toward something new, something deeper and higher. You are moving from where you have been into what God now has for you. I hope you like new things, because God has plenty of them for all of us.

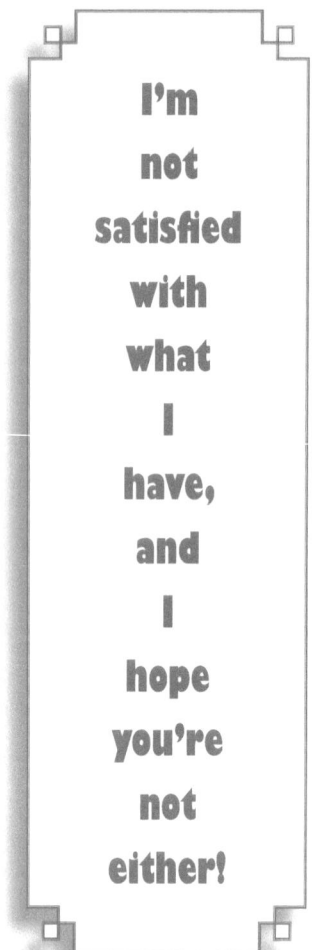

I'm not satisfied with what I have, and I hope you're not either!

Some people who are called to be launched into the deep have already been swimming in deep places. Still, God is calling them deeper. Some of us just haven't seen the full picture yet. Getting into deeper water may mean getting a fuller look.

When you launch out, your phone will start ringing more. You'll discover more people to whom you can minister. You will discover more gifts in yourself that you didn't know you had. In some cases, it may mean simply a higher level of what you're already experiencing. Whatever the case, God is about to favor you because He sees the desires of your heart.

God Sees Your Heart

God said in His Word:

For the eyes of the Lord run to and fro throughout the whole earth to show Himself strong in behalf of those whose hearts are blameless toward him. 2 Chronicles 16:9

I know that these words were spoken many thousands of years ago, and yet I believe that our greatest hour of destiny is upon us. I've been here on this earth now for something more than sixty years, and I've been a born-again and Spirit-filled Christian for more than forty of those years. They have been wonderful years, but I have a powerful sense in my spirit that the greatest hour of destiny is just now coming upon the face of the earth.

Now, today, at this very moment, the eyes of the Lord are going to and fro in the earth, and He is searching for those whose hearts are stayed on Him, those whose hearts are perfect toward Him. His desire is to come to them and to pour out His Spirit upon them.

These are men and women who are desiring Him and seeking Him. These are men and women who are willing to lay down their lives for Him. All they want is to be of service to His Kingdom. All they want is to do exactly what the Spirit of God tells them to do and to say exactly what the Spirit of God tells them to say. When God finds such people, He shows Himself strong on their behalf.

God wants to *"show Himself strong"* on our behalf. I need that, and I'm sure you do too. I'm not satisfied with what I have, and I hope you're not either. We need and we want the fullness of God's presence and power.

The Bible declares:

For in him the whole fulness of the Deity (the Godhead) continues to dwell in bodily form [giving complete expression of the divine nature]. And you are in Him, made full and having come to fullness of life [in Christ you too are filled with the Godhead — Father, Son and Holy Spirit — and reach full spiritual stature]. And He is the Head of all rule and authority [of every angelic principality and power]. Colossians 2:9-10

So the *"fullness"* dwells in Him, and because we are in Him, the fullness should also dwell in us. It is the fullness of His power, of His authority and of His anointing. I'm not satisfied to have just a little, when He's ready to show Himself *"strong"* on my behalf and give me of His *"fullness."*

Are you a candidate for these blessings to-day? His eyes are searching. Let Him see your willingness.

Be Found Moving in the Right Direction

This is such an important time in the Kingdom of God that I personally feel I cannot afford to take even a single step in the wrong direction. I have to know, moment by moment, that I'm doing God's will. I cannot afford to take one step that is out of sync. I must not move ahead of where I'm supposed to be, and I also cannot be behind God's schedule for my life. There was never a more important hour than this one.

God has seen your heart. He knows your prayers and intercessions, your fasting, your pleas to Him, your crying out to His Spirit for direction, for understanding and revelation. And He wants to assure you that He is all of that and more. He is your wisdom, your counsel, your knowledge, your revelation, and your understanding.

He is truth. He is the direction you need. He will cause you to put one foot in front of the other and know the correct placement of them and exactly where you are to go and not to go, how to do it, when to do it, and also when not to do it. He is looking for those whom He can bless in this way.

Egypt as a Prophetic Representation

Moses and the children of Israel in Egypt were a prophetic representation of us all. We came out of Egypt the day we were born again and God delivered us with a mighty right hand. But today, right now, something wonderful is about to happen. The thing that has held you back and hindered your progress — the world system, the spirit of Pharaoh, the spirit of Egypt, whatever you want to call it — is about to loose its hold on you. God is ready to release you from every bondage and to thrust you out into your destiny.

The children of Israel were about to be thrust out of a position they had been in for the past four hundred and thirty years, What a sudden and dramatic change it was to be! Some of you may feel that your situation has drug on about that same length of time, but know that your change is coming too. Get ready to see *His Wonders in the Deep.*

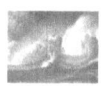

CHAPTER 9

NO TIME FOR DELAYS

They baked unleavened cakes of the dough which they brought from Egypt; it was not leavened because they were driven from Egypt and COULD NOT DELAY, nor had they prepared for themselves any food. Now the time the Israelites dwelt in Egypt was 430 years. At the end of the 430 years, even that very day, all the host of the Lord went out of Egypt. Exodus 12:39-41

For four hundred and thirty years, the Israelites had been in bondage in Egypt. Interestingly enough, their time in that land had started out well.

God Himself Sent the Children of Israel to Egypt

In fact, the children of Israel had been sent to Egypt by God Himself. He allowed a famine to come upon the land where Jacob and his sons lived, and He sent Joseph to Egypt ahead of them to prepare the way for their coming. This had all been done in an effort to preserve the people as a peculiar nation dedicated to the one true God.

At first, the descendants of Abraham, Isaac, and Jacob prospered under the care of Joseph, but as time went by, their prosperity became a threat to their hosts, the Egyptians. And, as the Egyptian rulers changed and the greatness of Joseph became a fading memory, it seemed wise to the Egyptians to place their "guests" into slavery, for they now feared them.

Why the Israelites allowed this to happen can only be imagined. Surely they must have become much too comfortable in Egypt, a type of the world, and they must have forgotten their spiritual heritage. It is not unusual for God's people to resort to Egypt, but woe to those who do.

Now the people were desperate to get out of Egypt, and God was about to bring them out. The key word here is *driven*. It means "thrust out" or "launched forth." This was a violent thing that was about to happen to them. Their life was about to be turned upside down (for the better), and they would never be the same again.

They Took
Unleavened Bread

I find it very interesting that the children of Israel took bread with them when they left Egypt, and yet it was free of leaven. There may be two reasons for this: For one thing, they just didn't have time to leaven their bread. But, I'm convinced that it was more than this, There was a purpose for it.

Leaven is a symbol of sin, of the world, and of death, and the children of Israel didn't want anything to hinder or delay them along the way or stop their deliverance. They were a people with a mission.

There was no time for delays in that moment, and the same is true today. Therefore the Israelites made sure that

Surely they must have become much too comfortable in Egypt, a type of the world, and they must have forgotten their spiritual heritage!

3

their bread did not contain the smallest amount of leaven. There could be no representation of sin and nothing of the world that could cause the hand of God to be withheld from them. The stakes were just too high, and, again, the same is true today. The launch window the Israelites enjoyed was too narrow for them to play games with it. They had to be serious with God, and so do we today.

What about you? I may not know exactly where God is taking you, but I can imagine that you feel like I do these days. I don't want anything to get in my way or, in any sense, to delay me. I'm on a mission. I'm being launched for a purpose, so I can't afford to let anything or anyone stand in my way. Just as in the day when the children of Israel prepared to leave Egypt, God is preparing to do a quick work in each of us, so there is no time for delays.

Is a Little Bit of Sin All that Bad?

Is a little bit of sin all that bad? Well, have you seen what leaven does to a lump of dough? It looks harmless at first, but then the lump begins to swell, and eventually the whole lump is affected. And that's exactly what happens to us through sin. It seems innocent enough at first, but in the end it affects everything about us, and it affects everyone in our lives.

4

You're on the launch platform, and God will very soon violently and swiftly thrust you out into your destiny, so don't let anything delay or hinder you. This means that you must guard yourself against all leaven, all possible sinful contamination.

Again, leaven seems like such an insignificant thing, but a little bit of it goes a long way. It permeates and affects everything it touches. Don't take that risk. Keep your bread unleavened. Keep your soul free from sin.

It's Time

It's time that we laid ourselves in the presence of God and cried out to Him to free us from anything and everything that might hinder our ministries in the future. He is more than sufficient to supply our every need in this regard. Let us take hold of the horns of the altar and hold on until the answer comes, until we are free of all leaven.

Each of us has some leaven that needs to be excised so that the whole lump is not destroyed. There is no time for further delay, so we must quickly get hold of God in this matter.

There is no good time for sin, for sin is distracting anytime, and it will always hold you back. Any little bit of leaven in your life will delay your ultimate destiny. As the Scriptures

> If we want what God has for us, we must be there to get it when it becomes available!

say, *"A little leaven will ferment the whole lump [of dough]"* (1 Corinthians 5:6). If you're not convinced of that fact, just look at what happened to Abraham.

Abraham's Launch Was Delayed

God told Abraham to leave his home and to travel toward a place He would show him, and there He would make of him a great nation. This journey of faith, Abraham was told, was very personal, and he was not to take anyone with him outside of his immediate family and servants. This calling was not for cousins, aunts and uncles, or grandparents. Abraham failed to obey God fully in this matter, for he took with him his nephew Lot, and also His father Terah. This was a grave mistake, for the name Terah means "delay," and Abraham was about to experience some serious delays.

Taking others along was just the opposite of what God

had told Abraham to do. This journey was his calling, not the calling of others. Others would only cause unnecessary delay. God had given Abraham specific instructions for his launch, but because he insisted on taking Terah with him, he would suffer many delays along the way and would reach his final destination only after much travail.

It's impossible to put too much emphasis on obedience to God. Obedience, the Scriptures declare, is *"better than sacrifice"* (1 Samuel 15:22). I'm sure that if Abraham had obeyed God fully in this matter, he would have found the land he sought much sooner.

This is a lesson for all of us, for Abraham is our father. We don't need any unnecessary delays in our lives. When God is moving, we can't afford to be out of step with Him. If we lose even one day, we may find ourselves too far behind to catch up. If we want what God has for us, we must be there to get it when it becomes available.

God Was Silent

Soon after leaving Ur, Abraham noticed something very frightening. God wasn't speaking to him as He had before. And this went on for the next two years. In many ways, it's difficult to imagine just what Abraham went through during this silent period. Not only was he in a strange, barren, and dangerous place, but he was now apparently alone, and he wasn't making any progress.

When we're living in disobedience, it's difficult to get direction from God. Therefore we lack understanding and wisdom. We desperately need to hear the voice of God, and we need His revelation knowledge. But at times like this, God is suddenly silent.

Until that time, God had given Abraham specific direction, but now, as he was wandering across the wilderness toward he didn't know what, he wasn't hearing from God anymore — not even a word. That was extremely dangerous.

They were in a place called Haran, a name that means "a very dry place, parched by the sun." So, for two years, Abraham sat in the heat of this desert area, and he listened for the voice of God, but it did not come as in former times. Not a word! Not a note! Nothing ... until Terah (delay) eventually died:

And Terah lived 205 years; and Terah died in Haran.　　　　　Genesis 11:32

Terah actually lived longer then Sarah did. She only lived to be a hundred and twenty-one, but Terah lived to be two hundred and five.

Finally Terah, Abraham's delay, passed from this life. This had to happen before Abram could become Abraham, before this godly and humble man could become what he was destined to become from the foundations of the world. Delay had kept him from it for a season, and so delay, Terah, had to die.

Delay Was Removed

The death of Terah could not have been an easy thing for Abraham. He suffered greatly because of it, but almost immediately God began to speak to him again and to give him direction for his life. In the very next verses of the Bible we read:

Now [in Haran] the Lord said to Abram, Go for yourself [for your own advantage] away from your country, from your relatives and your father's house, to the land that I will show you. And I will make of you a great nation, and I will bless you [with abundant increase of favors] and make your name famous and distinguished, and you will be a blessing [dispensing good to others]. And I will bless those who bless you [who confer prosperity or happiness upon you] and curse him who curses or uses insolent language toward you; in you all the families and

kindred of the earth will be blessed [and by
you they will bless themselves].

Genesis 12:1-3

So, once the cause of the delay was removed, Abraham's life got back on course.
This makes me know that sometimes the
delays that we all seem to suffer from time
to time (and that sometimes seem to hang
around forever) will eventually be removed —
if we do the right thing. Suddenly, Abraham
was again receiving direction from the Lord,
and he was about to be thrust forth, launched
for God.

ABRAHAM'S VISITATION

I love the portion of scripture that speaks
of the visitation of angels with Abraham. They
asked him:

Is there anything too hard or too wonderful
for the Lord?   Genesis 18:14

The answer, of course, is that there's nothing too hard for Him. We can only imagine what
He has in store for us just around the bend.
Knowing this, there is no time for delay. And
because there's no time for delay in your life,
you cannot allow leaven to enter in. Get ready

for your spiritual journey, and expect God to do something supernatural for you.

In Egypt, centuries later, the Israelites would be *"driven"* from the land. Their going forth would be violent and immediate. And when it came, they could not afford to allow anything to prevent, or delay, their departure.

Not All Delays Are Bad

As we have seen, not all delays are bad. On the space shuttle launch pad, there were some aborted takeoffs, and that can happen to any of us. When it does, don't worry about it. God wants everything to be right for your advancement. Pay attention to detail, and within no time, you'll be ready to be launched into the deep.

Sometimes, when there was an aborted takeoff, the problems that caused it could be quickly addressed, and the rocket would be fired the very next day. Sometimes, if there were more extensive repairs to be made, the launch might be delayed longer. The delay was never any longer than was absolutely necessary. It was important to get that vessel launched and allow it to fulfill the purpose for which it was created.

Personally, I'm tired of delays and will not be satisfied until I have God's very best for my life.

By avoiding things that we know might cause a delay, we can assure that we will more quickly be launched forth to see *His Wonders in the Deep.*

CHAPTER 10

BEING EXPATRIATED

Then they wept aloud again; and Orpah kissed her mother-in-law [good-bye], but Ruth clung to her. Ruth 1:14

When you are being launched, there comes a thrust that propels you off of the launchpad, for, as we have seen, to be launched is to be thrust out or thrust forth. This word *thrust,* however, also means "to be expatriated," separated from your homeland and people. What does that mean to us as Christians?

1

Without Warning

> One moment, we're wondering what God has for us in the future, and the next moment, the future is here, and we can't seem to recognize it!

Sometimes we seem to be very well connected with family, friends and local church, and our lives seem to be running very smoothly. Then, without warning, the Spirit of God moves upon us, and we find ourselves moved out of our place. For some time, we have been committed to a certain group of people, usually family, friends or fellow believers, and we have been very dedicated to our particular locality and its future. But now we seem to be stumbling into something altogether new and strange.

One moment, we're wondering what God has for us in the future, and the next moment, the future is here, and we can't seem to recognize it. We also can't seem to recognize ourselves. We have changed; we've been expatriated.

What has happened? One moment we were totally loyal and committed, and the next moment we find that we cannot be loyal and committed to those same people, that same locality or that same cause any longer. Something has taken place on the inside of us, and we suddenly realize that we are forever changed.

I'm not talking about the way modern Christians jump from church to church or the way some children, once they are grown, cut all ties with their family. I'm talking about God calling you to a people who were formerly not your people.

What Are Patriots?

A patriot is not just someone who is patriotic. Each of us is a patriot, or citizen, of a certain country. We Americans are patriots of the United States of America; we're citizens of this great land. Many Americans are patriots by adoption, and that makes them expatriates of other countries. They have come here seeking a better life. It's one thing to do that by choice, and it's quite another thing to have it suddenly thrust upon you.

Most Americans would not like to be expatriated, at least for very long. But God wants to make us all expatriates, to thrust us forth into the great fields of His harvest all over the world.

At one point, God thrust me and my family out into another country, Mexico. We suddenly became expatriates, and people who had not been our people suddenly became our people. Many Americans become ill when they eat the food and drink the water of other countries. With me, it happened just the opposite. I wasn't sick while I was in Mexico, but when I would come home to Louisiana to visit, I would get sick. I had been expatriated, and although Louisiana was still part of my life, I could no longer make the same commitment to it. I had been launched into the deep. God had thrust me out. Suddenly, I found myself being dedicated to people I had previously known nothing about.

It may seem cruel to say it, but in order to be all that God has called us to be, each of us will have to be cut off from certain people, some of whom we love dearly.

A Permanent Change

Later, after we had moved back to this country, I expected to feel differently when we returned to Mexico, but it was not to be. In our next visit to that country, we experienced an awesome move of God and felt even more knit to the Mexican people. We enjoyed being with the pastor we had placed over the church and his wife and their children, now in their twenties. We enjoyed seeing how God had prospered them. But it was much more than that. I felt like lying on the ground in tears and crying out to God because I knew something was happening. We made a commitment to return later to conduct an evangelistic campaign. That pastor is now over fourteen churches and a Bible institute.

I might not have the right words to be able to express this well enough, but when you get launched out, when God puts you on the launch pad, you can be sure that when He has thrust you forth, there will be some expatriation taking place in your life. Some old familiar and comfortable things will be cut off, and other things will be changed.

This does not mean that everything has to change, but there will be some changes. Some things have to shift, and some things have to move, to get you from the point where you currently are to the next point to which God wants to take you.

Forced Out

Expatriated means "forced out, to force oneself or someone else to move away from one's own people or their own country." Some of you will be expatriated to other countries. Have you felt the missionary call? Get ready. It may be coming your way.

Not everyone will be sent out as a missionary. Sometimes there are things in our lives that God wants to change because of a new season that is upon us. He wants to thrust us forth, and that requires some separation. New seasons, new giftings, new ministries ... these all require change on our part.

You cannot stay where you are right now. This may mean a physical change for you, or it may mean a spiritual change. Whatever the case, change is inevitable. So don't fight it. Instead, embrace it.

You may be part of a very normal and otherwise healthy group of people, but if God is calling you, He might just have to separate you from them. He wants to launch you out, thrust you forth, because it's time to move you out into the deep. I'm sure that many of you are sensing this very thing in your spirit, and it's because God has something new for you.

Ruth Was Expatriated

But Naomi said to her two daughters-in-law, Go, return each of you to her mother's house. May the Lord deal kindly with you, as you have dealt with the dead and with me. The Lord grant that you may find a home and rest, each in the house of her husband! Then she kissed them and they wept aloud. And they said to her, No, we will return with you to your people.

But Naomi said, Turn back, my daughters, why will you go with me? Have I yet sons in my womb that may become your husbands? Turn back, my daughters, go; for I am too old to have a husband. If I should say I have hope, even if I should have a husband tonight and should bear sons, would you therefore wait till they were grown? Would you therefore refrain from marrying? No, my daughters; it is far more bitter for me than for you that the hand of the Lord is gone out against me.

Then they wept aloud again; and Orpah kissed her mother-in-law [good-bye], but Ruth clung to her.

Ruth 1:8-14

Some people can taste what God is about to do, and they will not be satisfied to stay in Moab!

7

Ruth of the Bible was an expatriate. She was actually a Moabite, and the Moabites had traditionally been enemies of God and of His people. It had been written that Moabites were cursed and could not enter the presence of God until ten generations had passed.

Moab was also considered to be a land of ease. I hope you're tired of living in ease, because God is ready to expatriate you and launch you forth. He will take you out of your ease and place you into a strategic corner of His harvest field.

Talk about being taken out of your comfort zone: Ruth was suddenly thrust out from everything she had ever known. She had married a Hebrew, the son of Naomi, but her father-in-law died, and then her husband died.

Naomi was a woman who was sensitive to the sounds of Heaven. Some people can hear what God is about to do, and they will not be satisfied to stay in Moab. In the same way, in the days to come, you will not be satisfied to linger where you have been day in and day out for years. As you hear the sounds of revival coming, you will be compelled to get into the move of God.

Naomi heard a sound that came from Bethlehem, Judea. The famine had ended, and God was feeding His people once again. Bethlchem means "house of bread," so God was feeding His people in the house of bread.

He was "in the house," as we have come to say in recent years. Revival had hit Bethlehem.

It was true. The famine had ended. Not only had revival come, not only was God feeding His people once again, but there was also a restoration in progress. The Midianites, the enemies of the Israelites, had been driven out, and God had lifted the curse and brought forth His hand of blessing once again upon the people and their land. As a result, something was stirring in Naomi's heart, and I'm sure that many of you could say the same today.

Naomi told Ruth that she should stay in Moab because she had no more sons to offer her, but she herself could not stay. There was no way she could restore the inheritance Ruth had lost with the death of her husband, so she imagined that her daughter-in-law would have to seek her future in some other way.

Stiff-Necked

Naomi had another widowed daughter-in-law, and her name was Orpah. Orpah means "stiff-necked." Ruth also has a meaning. It means "once belonging to the wrong side," but unlike Orpah, Ruth was now determined to come over to the right side.

When Orpah, like Ruth, was given her liberty to stay behind in her native Moab, she jumped at

> When we want more of God, it requires that we make some difficult choices! Making those difficult decisions is often what launches us out into the deep!

the chance. Because she was stiff-necked, she couldn't discern the seriousness of what God was about to do. Ruth, however, when presented with the same opportunity to abandon her mother-in-law, could not bring herself to do it. When she heard her mother-in-law talk about a move of God in the land of Judea, she found her heart mysteriously stirred. No matter what the cost to her, she was determined to stay with Naomi. She was willing to be thrust out from her people and the place she had known her entire life, and she was ready for a whole new environment, a whole new life-style, a whole new way of doing things, a whole new way of operating.

Ruth Would Have to Change

Nothing that Ruth had known or done as a Moabite could come with her into the place she was now going. This was a brand new day. She was being thrust out, expatriated, so she had to change.

Each of us must make a decision about certain things in our lives, what we will cling to and what we are willing to leave behind. Change is not always an easy thing, and most of us don't like it much, if at all. But, in God, change is necessary and good.

It's surprising how many people don't like change and how much they don't like it, but if we don't accept change, we can never have God's best for our lives. Get ready for change, because it's bound to come. And the reason is that the call of God is mighty upon our lives.

When we want more of God, it requires that we make some difficult choices. Making those difficult decisions is often what launches us out into the deep. We begin taking steps we've never taken before, going places we've never gone before, and doing things we've never done before. We leave some old things behind, and we leave some old friends behind, and that sounds very painful. But when we allow God to replace everything we have sacrificed, He gives us so much more than we ever had before.

We must each know that what God has in store for us is always much greater than anything we could sacrifice for Him that it can hardly be called "sacrifice" in the traditional sense of the word. Our obedience to the Lord is always followed by wonderful blessings. Good words to describe God's intentions toward you are "more," "better," and "greater." Don't listen to the enemy who will paint sacrifice in other, very different terms.

When God places something in our hearts and minds, what should we do? We should step out on it, trusting Him to help us. He has promised to meet us at the point of our obedience and to bless us there. His hand will surely be upon all that we do as we walk in obedience to Him.

God has called some of us to preach His Word, to teach, to prophesy, to lay hands on the sick and bring them healing, and to raise the dead. And when His call is upon us, we can know that it will be accompanied by His anointing. This brings about great change, and we're never the same again. But this kind of change is always good.

A Serious Decision to Make

Ruth had a serious decision to make. She was being asked to accept something that she knew nothing about. She only had the stirring in her heart. It told her that something important was happening in Bethlehem. There was revival there. Based on that sensing, Ruth made her decision. Her response was: "Wherever Naomi goes that's where I'm going. I feel something in my spirit, and I'm going to go for it."

Naomi was very cautious with Ruth. She didn't want her to later regret her decision:

And Naomi said, See, your sister-in-law has gone back to her people and to her gods: return after your sister-in-law.

Ruth 1:15

But it no longer mattered what Naomi said. Ruth had made a decision in her heart, and she could not go back on it. Even if Orpah went back to her life of ease, her Moab, and even if she went back to her false gods, Ruth would never go back.

Orpah's decision would prove to be fatal. Because she was stiff-necked, what she was about to do would define her total future existence. She would, from this day forward, be marked. Her fate was sealed. She would find another Moabite to marry, and she would settle into a life of ease, but it would also be a life without God and a life without spiritual revival.

God had been ready to deliver her and to give her a totally new existence, but she could not see her way clear to accept His offer. It seemed too risky to her, like a foolish move. She had to do what was, for her, more "safe." Sadly, far too many of God's people are just like that.

Ruth Protested

When urged to follow the lead of her sister-in-law, Ruth protested:

Urge me not to leave you or to turn back from following you; for where you go I will go, and where you lodge, I will lodge. Your people shall be my people and your God my God.

Ruth 1:17

This was Ruth's decision. She was ready to follow her mother-in-law because of what she felt in her spirit.

How about you? God may not be sending you to some Third-World country, but He definitely does want to thrust you out into the deep.

To many, Orpah's decision would have seemed safe and wise. After all, Ruth didn't know where she would lay her head the next moment. But that didn't matter. She knew what was in her heart and in her spirit, and she sensed that she had made the best decision.

Ruth was so convinced that she was doing the right thing that she further said to Naomi:

Where you die I will die, and there will I be buried. The Lord do so to me, and more also, if anything but death parts me from you.

Ruth 1:7

That's powerful! Ruth was forging an un-breakable covenant relationship with her mother-in-law. If you've ever wondered why God would make Ruth one of the ancestors of Jesus, here's your answer. She was a serious woman. And Ruth was not just making a covenant with Naomi; she was making a covenant with Naomi's God.

THE RETURN TO BETHLEHEM

Ruth's words must have made Naomi very happy:

When Naomi saw that Ruth was determined to go with her, she said no more. So they both went on until they came to Bethlehem.
Ruth 1:18-19

It soon became apparent to the people in Bethlehem that Naomi had suffered a lot:

Naomi was not without blame in what she had suffered, for she had made some wrong decisions in life!

And when they arrived in Bethlehem, the whole town was stirred about them, and said, Is this Naomi?

*And she said to them, Call me not Naomi
[pleasant]; call me Mara [bitter], for the
Almighty has dealt very bitterly with me. I
went out full, but the Lord has brought me
home again empty. Why call me Naomi,
since the Lord has testified against me, and
the Almighty has afflicted me.*

Ruth 1:19-21

Since leaving Bethlehem, Naomi's life had
clearly been filled with bitterness. We can feel
her pain as she declared that her name should
be changed to Mara. But she was not without
blame in what she had suffered. Naomi had
made some wrong decisions in life, principally
the decision to leave God's land, His appointed
place for her life, and turn away to a life of
ease.

As always, there had seemed to be a good
reason for this at the time. There was famine
in Israel, while in Moab, it was said, there was
plenty. But in the process of seeking the mate-
rial rather than the spiritual, ten full years of
Naomi's life had been lost, wasted. She and her
husband, Elimalech, had tithed their lives into
Moab, giving ten years to something that was
not of God and brought them only a curse.

As a result, God had dealt harshly with
Naomi. First, He allowed her husband to die,
and then both of her sons died. Now, however,

she had a new hope. It was a new season, and God had new blessings awaiting her:

So Naomi returned, and Ruth the Moabitess, her daughter, with her, who returned from the country of Moab. And they came to Bethlehem at the beginning of barley harvest.   Ruth 1:22

They left the land of ease and came to the house of bread, and it just happened to be harvest time. Isn't that wonderful? And when God thrusts you out, you will also discover that it's harvest time. That's precisely why He's thrusting you out. Like Ruth, who was expatriated when she allowed God to take her to a people who were before not her people, you will be a partaker of the harvest.

SAUL WAS EXPATRIATED

Saul (as he was originally known) or Paul (as he came to be known to the whole world) was also expatriated. It happened one day as he was on his way to Damascus. Before his encounter with Christ on the road that day, Paul had been a serious persecutor of everything Christian. He accused Christians, he had them imprisoned, he gave testimony against them, and he had them put to death. He hated Christ and all Christians, and he was determined to stop this movement — even if he had to do it single-handedly. That was ... until the hand of the Lord came upon him.

He was traveling along that day, minding his own business, when suddenly he was confronted by the Spirit of God. And when the Spirit of God touches your life, it doesn't matter what you've done or what direction you happen to be going in at the moment. You are destined for expatriation.

Saul was so totally changed by his encounter with Christ that day on the road to Damascus that no one dared to call him by the same name again. He was now Paul. He was no longer a Jew among Jews; he was about to become the first apostle to the Gentiles. This was very strange, because until that moment Paul had wanted nothing to do with Gentiles.

This transformation did not come without a struggle of sorts. Paul was blinded, an extremely drastic step that we don't often see repeated in the Scriptures. God was determined to get Saul's attention, and it worked. This Pharisee of the Pharisees now became what he had hated, a born-again Christian believer, and a man who would spend the rest of his life reaching out to Gentiles all over the world with the message of Christ.

In those days, when Jews said the word *Gentile,* they nearly spit it out. It was a hated term. The Gentiles definitely lived on the wrong side of the tracks, and every Jew was glad he wasn't a Gentile. Now a great change came to Saul, one he hadn't seen coming. He had been on his way to Damascus to do more mischief against the Christians, for he was obsessed with wiping them out, but God had his number.

No longer a Jew among Jews, hating the Gentiles, whom he believed to be defiled, Saul (now Paul) was expatriated from everything he had believed to be right and for which he had sacrificed to take an unswerving stand, to a whole new way of thinking, believing, and acting. Those who were once his people would no longer be his people, and his commitment would now lie with those he had once persecuted.

Are you ready to be expatriated to another city, country or people, either to be forced out or to leave of your own fee will for a divine purpose? Get ready. God needs men and women of every age group and of every talent to do His bidding today all around the world. Allow Him to carry you out so that you can see and experience *His Wonders in the Deep.*

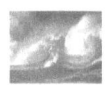

CHAPTER 11

THE MANDATES OF GOD

Now the word of the Lord came to Jonah son of Amittai, saying, Arise, go to Ninevah, that great city, and proclaim against it, for their wickedness has come up before Me.

Jonah 1:1-2

Another Bible character who had an experience with the deep was Jonah. Jonah was under a mandate from God, and when we respond to His mandates, that's when we can see His power manifested in our lives.

This is a serious issue, for if we fail to respond to the mandate of God upon our lives, we will never be able to be what He has destined us

1

to be, and we will never be able to do what He has destined us to do. His power comes upon those who dedicate themselves to do His will.

My Heavenly Mandate

One day I was having lunch with my friend and traveling companion, Cindy Stevens. As the two of us were sitting there eating and talking, God visited me in such a powerful way that I have never been able to forget it. The Spirit of the Lord broke in upon my mind, and with great clarity, showed me what I must do.

I had often pondered about what I was doing at the time: weekly meetings in a number of nearby towns where we gathered people from the area who were hungry for more of God and ministered to them and regular conferences in which we gathered larger crowds to worship, share the revelation of God's Word, and receive from His hand. It was all grand and powerful, and impressive fruit was being produced for the Kingdom, and yet I had often wondered if this was indeed God's very best for us.

When the Spirit of the Lord broke in upon me that day, His first words to me were these: "What you are doing is a mandate from Heaven; it is a command." I knew immediately that He was showing me that what I was doing was not an option, not something that I could do or not do as I chose.

It was a clear and precise mandate from Heaven that I knew I simply must obey. There was no alternative.

As soon as I could after I got home, I looked up the word *mandate* in *Webster's Dictionary*. The very first meaning listed was "a command." It also showed that a mandate came "from a higher up." It was as if I was being hired by God, and the command was coming down from Him. What was very obvious was that I was a subordinate, and there was Someone in a higher position who was giving the orders.

Now any of us who has ministered for any length of time knows this, but the reality of it through the meaning of the word *mandate* made it precisely clear. I had long known that I was a subordinate, hired by the Lord Himself, but now a reality that could not be denied had come. This gave me a wonderful sense of peace.

What the Lord showed me that day was not an option! It was a clear and precise mandate from Heaven!

3

I also saw that the word *mandate* meant that if I was hired by someone in a higher position, and I had received from them a mandate, I was guaranteed never to suffer loss in executing it. That, too, was an exciting revelation.

What Is God's Mandate Over Your Life?

What is God's mandate over your life? I am convinced that there is such a mandate for each of us. When the voice of the Lord goes forth, what He has spoken is not an option; it is a command.

Too many times in the past we have not been faithful to the Lord's mandates, and that is a serious matter. I pray that the Lord will bring to your remembrance the things He has spoken to you to do in the past and help you to fulfill them.

We are sometimes tempted to think that such a mandate was a figment of our own imaginations. *"Surely the Lord would not call me to do such great things. I'm so comfortable right where I am. Why try to walk on water?"* we reason.

I Am About to Break in Upon Men's Lives

One day, as I was seeking the Lord, I was taken up by the Spirit, and I saw the earth and

4

those who were in it going about their day-to-day lives, not understanding, nor even being aware of the things God was preparing to do in the earth. Then the Lord said to me, "I am about to break in upon men's lives. The people of this world have no concept of the great things of Heaven or of the Kingdom of God. They cannot know the things that are soon to come that will shake their worlds." Nineveh, too, was about to feel God's touch.

"ARISE, GO TO NINEVEH!"

Jonah was under the mandate of the Lord. The Lord had given him specific direction for what he was to do, and it was a command, not an option. Jonah could not choose to stray from what God had commanded him to do and still expect to prosper. He could not stray either to the right or to the left. The mandate was very specific. He had to do exactly what God had commissioned him to do. God had spoken, and Jonah must obey.

The problem was that God was asking Jonah to go to a place known as Nineveh, and Nineveh was not a very nice place. In fact, As a city, Nineveh was in the category of Sodom and Gomorrah. But there were also in Nineveh *"more than 120,000 persons not [yet old enough to] know their right hand from their left"* (Jonah

4:11), and God did not want to bring destruction upon the city because of them, so He had sent Jonah to warn these people of the impending destruction and give them a chance to escape it.

When God called Jonah, it was to bring the Ninevites to repentance, but Jonah was not very happy about God's mandate, and he went the other way. He left the presence of the Lord:

But Jonah rose up to flee to Tarshish from being in the presence of the Lord [as His prophet] and went down to Joppa and found a ship going to Tarshish [the most remote of the Phoenician trading places then known]. So he paid the appointed fare and went down into the ship to go with them to Tarshish from being in the presence of the Lord [as His servant and minister].

Jonah 1:3

The divine mandates the Lord is whispering into our ears these days have been determined since before the foundations of the world!

We can understand Jonah's reluctance to go to Nineveh. The name *Nineveh* means "a habitation," but Nineveh was a habitation of wickedness. It was a dwelling place or a habitation of sin. Jonah knew that once the people of Nineveh learned that he was a prophet of God, they would surely try to kill him. Still, God loved that wicked city and its inhabitants and sent Jonah to bring His message to them.

Today, the whole earth, it seems, has become one great Sodom and Gomorrah, a modern-day Nineveh. But this is not a reason to turn our backs on hurting people. It is, in fact, the very reason the Lord is mandating our participation in the salvation of the earth. According to our giftings and callings, He is sending us forth.

May God cause our ears to be sensitive to His voice in this hour. May He help us to tune our ears to the sounds of Heaven. May our God impress upon us in this hour the need for obedience. It is obedience that will save us from perilous times, from the tempestuous storms of life. It is obedience that will keep us in all things.

The divine mandates the Lord is whispering into our ears these days have been determined since before the foundations of the world. They have been held in reserve, waiting for the appropriate time. This, now, is the time of the Lord's visitation upon our lives. Rise up and go quickly.

An Unexpected Message

This word *proclaim* is very interesting. It meant that God wanted Jonah to go to the people when they least expected it and present something totally new to them. His message was unexpected and, again today, the people of this world are not expecting what God is about to do. They are not expecting the proclamation of the Word of God that will soon come forth in the earth. It will accost them because they have no way of anticipating it, just as no one was expecting a prophet to appear and speak the words Jonah brought.

Proclaim means "to meet someone face to face when they least expect it." It means "to confront." As divine destiny is loosed upon the earth, the world will be taken by surprise. Modern men and women are consumed with the things of this world, but God is about to turn their world upside down. He was saying to Jonah, "Go to them when they least expect it. Go and confront them."

Jonah, I believe, is a type of the Church, and God is preparing to loose His Jonahs in the earth today. He will do it when the world is least expecting it. Suddenly, He will break in upon men and women and confront them. It's time to go and proclaim His Word.

The men and women of this world are about to come face to face with God when they least expect it. They are about to be confronted. They are soon to have an encounter with the Creator. Hear your Jonah call today.

When God sends us to proclaim His Word to the world, and He confronts the people of the world when they least expect it, it will be because of His mercy. He had mercy upon Nineveh, and He has mercy upon the world today. He knows the wickedness of men's hearts, and yet He extends to them His arms of love.

JONAH'S DECISION

When Jonah made the decision to avoid the Lord's mandate and to go the other way, this didn't mean that he was lost (although some may feel like it when they disobey God). It didn't mean that Jonah was on his way to Hell (although, to him, it may have felt like he was already there). It did mean that Jonah had left *"the presence of the Lord,"* and that's always a dangerous prospect for anyone, especially a prophet.

We don't want to leave our Lord ever. He is the Alpha and the Omega, the Beginning and the End. He is the First and the Last. He knew you before the foundations of the earth, and He formed you in your mother's womb. He knows where you've come from, He knows where you presently are, and He knows where you're going. He knows exactly how your life will end.

Every great man and woman in the Bible had a humble beginning. But, although their beginnings were not impressive, by God's mercy and grace, they had great endings. Even Abraham, the father of faith, came from a family of idolators. He certainly didn't begin as the father of faith, but that's how he ended his life.

We're all different, we all have different giftings, different callings and diversities of administrations. We don't look alike, and we don't act alike. And it's good that we don't. But whatever your particular calling, receive God's unique mandate for your life, and then be faithful to it.

Jonah Fled from the Presence of God

Jonah went to Joppa, and there he found a ship going to Tarshish. Of all places, why did he pick Tarshish? The Scriptures say that it was *"the most remote of the Phoenician trading places then known."* Isn't it interesting that when we willingly choose to disobey God, before long we have drifted off to some far place that God never intended us to be? This was foreign soil, but that's what Jonah knowingly chose.

The name *Tarshish* means "delightful and pleasant." It means "to set affections on." *Surely God wants me to be in Tarshish,* we somehow think. *It would feel so much better being there. It is such a delightful place, so pleasant. I could really set my affections on a place like that.*

Far too many times we go to the spiritual Tarshishes of this world, and we quickly get our affections set on the wrong things. We so easily enter onto foreign soil that the Lord never intended for us to even visit, let alone embrace.

PAYING THE PRICE

The Bible says clearly that Jonah *"paid the appointed fare."* There is always a price to pay for disobedience to God's mandate. This word *price* can mean that he paid "a wage." It can mean that he hired himself out. If that

Surely God wants me to be in Tarshish, we somehow think. It would feel so much better being there!

is the meaning here, then Jonah had hired himself out to the wrong person. Have you ever done that?

Jesus said:

My meat is to do the will of him that sent me, and to finish his work.

John 4:34, KJV

Oh, that each of us would be careful to follow our Lord's example! Jesus was saying that doing the will of the Father was what He did best, and that's true of all of us.

Jonah was about to pay a heavy price for leaving God's presence and for avoiding His mandate.

It Should Frighten Us All

The story of Jonah should frighten all of us enough that we shake ourselves and start doing what we're called to do. Gird up the loins of your mind, and get busy fulfilling your call. There is no other acceptable option. You must go and you must do, because the Almighty God has said so. You have a divine mandate upon your life.

We're all human enough to understand Jonah's reaction. At times, the call of God on our lives is so overwhelming that it seems easier for us to cross over to some foreign soil, some place of ease and delight, than to face the thing God had commissioned us to do. But now the time is so late that we cannot afford to waste our years running to our Tarshishes. These are serious times, times that demand a serious commitment on our part, a commitment to God's very best for our lives.

God Has a Way of Forcing Us to Get Serious

If we fail to get serious, God has ways of making us serious:

> *But the Lord sent out a great wind upon the sea, and there was a violent tempest upon the sea so that the ship was about to be broken.*   Jonah 1:4

We cannot run from the voice of God and expect to avoid the storms of His wrath. Therefore, when you find yourself in the midst of some storm, examine your heart to see if you have perhaps brought it upon yourself. Is your storm caused by the enemy trying to discourage you from proceeding? Or is it caused by the Lord because you are running from His perfect will? He often uses storms to get our attention.

What
Jonah
was
experiencing
in
that
moment
probably
didn't
feel
very
good,
but
his
answer
was
on
the
way!

The Word of God shows us that we *"perish for lack of knowledge"* (KJV):

My people are destroyed for lack of knowledge.

Hosea 4:6

God's Word contains many holy principles, and if we obey those principles, we will be blessed. If we disobey, we will suffer the consequences. Jonah didn't have to go through that storm, but it was good for him anyway.

It Was a Terrifying Storm

It was indeed a terrifying storm:

Then the mariners were afraid, and each man cried to his god; and they cast the goods that were in the ship into the sea to lighten it for them. But Jonah had gone down into the inner part of the ship and had lain down and was fast asleep. So the captain came and said to him, What do you mean, you sleeper? Arise, call upon your God! Perhaps your God will give a thought to us so that we shall not perish.   Jonah 1:5-6

This word *arise* means "to repent, make things right, to be strengthened." It can also be used in the sense of "arise to your rightful position." If we're going in the wrong direction, something needs to happen to get us turned around and going the right way again.

When the captain of the ship commanded Jonah, *"Arise and call upon your God,"* the prophet was being told to repent, make things right, be strengthened, and restored to his rightful position and then have an encounter with God before they all perished. What Jonah was experiencing in that moment probably didn't feel very good, but his answer was on the way. The storm had forced him to seek God.

THE STORY MIGHT HAVE BEEN VERY DIFFERENT

If Jonah had done what God had told him to do in the first place and had gone to Nineveh, instead of Tarshish, the story would have been quite different. Some of you need to have a fresh encounter with the Lord. You can't go on your experiences of last year or six months ago. I can't even go on my experiences or encounters with God from last week. Today presents us with a whole new set of circumstances, so we must pray today and be totally surrendered and dependent upon the Lord today — and then again tomorrow. We must have a daily encounter with Him.

Like Jonah, the church is prophetically a sleeping giant, and she needs to arise out of her sleeping condition. At last, Jonah woke up, but things around him were getting worse by the moment, and he was soon enough identified as the cause of it all:

> *And they each said to one another, Come, let us cast lots, that we may know on whose account this evil has come upon us. So they cast lots and the lot fell on Jonah.* Jonah 1:7

The casting of lots was a common practice of that day and was even used by the priests of Israel. When there was sin in the camp, the priests would gather the people and begin to cast lots to find out who the offender was. First the lot would fall on the particular tribe where the sin was located. Then the priests would cast lots again, and this time the lot would fall on a particular family in that tribe. It was done a third time, and the lot would fall on the exact individual who had committed the sin, and he would be punished, so that God's wrath could be averted.

Jonah Is Confronted

In Jonah's case, as the men on board the ship began to cast lots, the lot fell on him. Just that quickly it became evident that God knew where he was all along. Everything that is done in darkness will eventually come to light. Jonah was immediately confronted:

> *Then they said to him, Tell us, we pray you, on whose account has this evil come upon us. What is your occupation? Where did you come from? And what is your country and nationality?*   Jonah 1:8

Once we have been bought by the blood of the Lamb, it is impossible to escape from who we are and what we are in His Kingdom. *"What is your occupation?"* Once you've been hired, you're hired, and there's no turning back.

"What is your country and nationality?" Once we belong to God, we're no longer of this earth. We're only strangers passing through. We're foreigners and aliens here. We don't belong.

I have been so spoiled by the riches of the Kingdom of God that there is no longer any

> When Jesus called him to walk on water, they were uncharted waters — for him at least. He had never walked on water before!

enticement to the things this world has to offer. As believers in Christ, the things of this earth have no hold over us.

Jonah Had Done a Shameful Thing

Jonah was not ashamed of his purpose in life, as a prophet, a minister, and a servant of God, but he had done something shameful that needed to be confessed. He had run from God's mandate upon his life:

And he said to them, I am a Hebrew, and I [reverently] fear and worship the Lord, the God of heaven, Who made the sea and the dry land.
Then the men were exceedingly afraid and said to him, What is this that you have done? For the men knew that he fled from being in the presence of the Lord [as His prophet and servant], because he had told them. Then they said to him, What

shall we do to you, that the sea may subside and be calm for us? For the sea became more and more [violently] tempestuous.

And [Jonah] said to them, Take me up and cast me into the sea; so shall the sea become calm for you, for I know that it is because of me that this great tempest has come upon you.   Jonah 1:9-12

When the men on board that ship knew that Jonah had disobeyed God, they *"were exceedingly afraid."* Isn't that interesting? Even the world will know when you have left the presence of the Lord. They will know if you're anointed or not.

Jonah's solution to the problem was amazing: *"Take me up and cast me into the sea."* In other words, he was saying, "THROW ME INTO THE DEEP." He was sure that the storm would immediately pass if they did this. And he was right. When you obey the mandates of God and launch out to the deep, your storm will suddenly cease.

We all know the story. Jonah was spared. The whale that swallowed him spit him out on dry land, and he went on to bring revival to Nineveh.

How about you? Are you ready to move out into deeper waters so that you can experience *His Wonders in the Deep?*

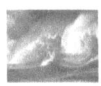

CHAPTER 12

THE LORD'S CONSTRAINT

And straightway Jesus constrained his disciples to get into a ship, and to go before him unto the other side, while he sent the multitudes away.   Matthew 14:22, KJV

After their calling, the disciples of Jesus had other encounters with the sea. For instance, after Jesus had fed the multitudes, He *"constrained"* them to get into a ship and cross the sea. Have you ever felt the constraining hand of God? When you are constrained, it means that you're not free; you're being compelled. How we respond in these moments is very important. If we resist the constraining arm of God, we place ourselves in rebellion against Him, and that's a very dangerous place to be.

The twelve men Jesus chose had begun as mere disciples, but they would eventually become mighty apostles!

The Next Step

Jesus had done many wonderful miracles that day, some of which we have recorded and others that were never recorded. We know that He had fed five thousand men, plus their women and children. With Him, as He did these things, were the twelve men whom He had chosen to carry on His work after Him. They had begun as mere disciples, but they would eventually become mighty apostles.

The multitudes had all been fed and many baskets full of bread and fish had been left over. The Word had gone forth, and great miracles had been done. But now, at the end of the day, when the disciples might have been expecting to rest, Jesus constrained them to get into a boat to cross the sea to the other side. The Bible assures us:

For the love of Christ constraineth us.

2 Corinthians 5:14, KJV

For the love of Christ controls and urges and impels us ... . AMP

To Persuade with Strong Pressure

This word *constrain* means "to persuade with strong pressure." So the disciples didn't have a choice in this matter. They were not free to choose where they would go or what they would do. They were forced to get into the ship that day, for they were about to embark on a God-ordained journey. It was to be quite an adventure for them.

Constraint means "to influence with a use of force to cause an action or prevent an action." The disciples had been with Jesus all day, and they had seen many miracles. Now the day was ending, and they were surely tired. Then Jesus spoke to them about taking a journey to the other side. And they were given no choice in the matter. Jesus *"constrained"* them.

To some, this may sound like a scary thing, but believe me, it's not. When God constrains us to go with Him, we should rejoice. His plans for us are wonderful, and when we yield to them, the results are always equally wonderful.

3

These days, many believers are having their lives turned upside down by the constraining hand of the Holy Spirit. He is urging us to do things we never would have dared to do. In a very real sense, He is pushing us out into deeper waters.

Restricted Liberties

That Jesus *"constrained"* the disciples means that He "persuaded them with strong pressure or use of force to influence or prevent an action." *Constraint* means "the state of being compelled to do or not to do something," and it speaks of "restricted liberties." The deeper your walk with God and the deeper His call becomes upon your life, the greater His constraints will be, and the less liberties you will have in this life.

Personally, I don't enjoy the same liberties I did ten or fifteen years ago. By that, I mean that I no longer have the choice of doing certain things I used to do. I have been *"constrained"* by the Holy Spirit.

I'm not talking about bad things. Some of the things we are called on to let go of are not bad in themselves, but they are time and energy wasters, and we can't afford to waste either these days. There is a harvest to be reaped, so get into the ship. Forget the other plans you've made, and go God's way. After all, *He* is Lord of this harvest.

CLEANSED

The root word from which we get our word *ship* is interesting and has several meanings. It does refer to a boat, but not just any boat. It refers to a ship that can "plunge through the water." This journey of the Spirit we are embarking on will be on a vessel that has this capacity.

When something is plunged through water, it is cleansed. This is an unusual aspect of the meaning of the word *ship*. It means "to cleanse the hands, feet and face." When we are constrained by the Holy Spirit, and we yield to that constraint upon our lives, we are suddenly plunged into the cleansing power of the blood of the Lamb of God. This cleansing is part of our call into the deep and part of the reason that we then see the wonders of God. When we surrender and get on His assigned ship for the journey, He delights in applying His cleansing power to our lives and giving us a fresh baptism.

The word *ship* also refers to a baptism in water. And what happens when we're baptized? The old man is left behind, and we come up out of the water as a new creation.

ORDAINED FOR THE SUPERNATURAL

God has not ordained us to live mundane lives. He has ordained us for the supernatural, and that can only be accomplished when we are constrained by His Spirit. When we choose to yield to His constraints, the old man is left behind in a process of cleansing. As we get on board the designated ship, and we feel the wind blowing against our faces, as the ship takes off for deeper waters, whatever remains of yesterday is then washed off of us. As the ship plunges into the deeper waters, the cleansing process also deepens, and the old you is totally washed away.

Some months ago I told the Lord I wanted Him to change me so fully that when I would look in the mirror I wouldn't even recognize myself. I didn't want to look or act like the same person. I didn't want to be what I then was. I wanted Him to change me from the inside out, so that I wouldn't even recognize myself. And God was faithful. He has called me into depths that I could only have imagined some years ago.

It is time to abandon the mundane life and to begin to operate in the depths of the Kingdom of God. It's time to become serious, so that we can see the wonders of God. He wants to hire you, employ you, and place His badge of deputyship on you so that everyone will know that you are a representative of the King of Glory.

IT MAY NOT FEEL GOOD

When you yield to the constraints of the Spirit and get aboard the ship that He has destined for you, it may not always feel good. After all, you don't know what to expect. You don't know what lies on the other side. And you don't know what might happen on your way across the waters. But if you will just say, "Lord, I yield to the constraints of Your Holy Spirit upon my life. I will go with the flow of what You are doing in me — even if I'm not sure I like it or even if it doesn't feel good at the moment," as that ship begins to plunge into deep waters, there will come a cleansing to you, a washing away of the old, and this will prepare you for the new.

Every one of us needs the cleansing power of God, and when it comes, it's like a new baptism of the Holy Spirit has come upon us.

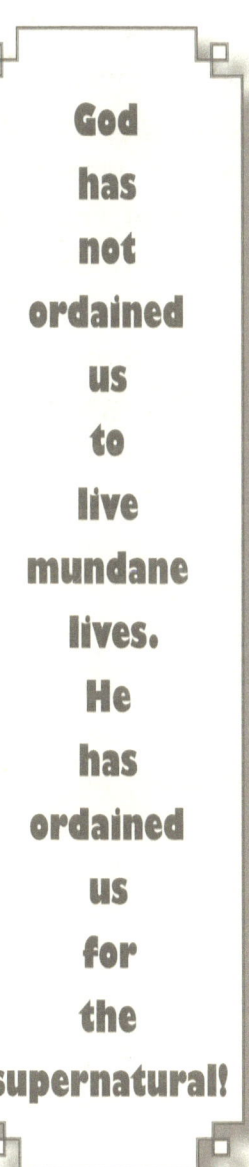

God has not ordained us to live mundane lives. He has ordained us for the supernatural!

CLEANSE THE WHOLE PERSON

This word *ship* also means "to cleanse the whole person, to wash the garments." Some of your garments need to be washed today. When Isaiah was confronted by the awesome presence of the Lord in the Temple, he suddenly realized that he was *"a man of unclean lips"* (Isaiah 6:5). If we are honest, most of us would have to say the same.

Things like anger, bitterness, disappointment, and confusion have sent words spilling out of our lips, and those words have not always been holy or edifying. Because of battles raging inside of us and against us, we have not always had the cleanest thoughts. Let us yield to the constraint of the Holy Spirit, get on board His ship, and move out into some deeper waters, so that we can do some serious business for God.

When Isaiah realized his uncleanness, a seraph was sent to bring a hot coal from the altar of God, to purge him. Let yourself be purged in deep waters today. Some of you have allowed the enemy to come into your beautiful garden and defile it. Be purged today, as you plunge through the waters of the deep. Some of you have willingly thrown open the gates and let the world in. It's time for a cleansing.

Do you long to see God and to see His wonders? Then get into the ship, while He sends the multitudes away, just as He did when He constrained His disciples to get into the ship that day. Great crowds will never follow Him into the deeper places, but He constrains you to walk there.

THE DISCIPLES IN TROUBLE

In obedience, having been constrained by the Lord, the disciples went before Jesus in the ship. Before long, however, they found themselves in trouble:

> *And when he had sent the multitudes away, he went up into a mountain apart to pray: and when the evening was come, he was there alone. But the ship was now in the midst of the sea, tossed with waves: for the wind was contrary.* Matthew 14:23-24, KJV

No doubt there are some winds blowing against your life right now that we could safely call *"contrary."* Don't be disconcerted by this, for it's part of God's plan. Before Jesus constrained the disciples to get on that ship, He knew that some contrary winds would blow against them. When it happened, He was not surprised by it, and neither was He alarmed. He knows all about the contrary winds blowing against your life too.

Jesus Was There

> The
> wonderful
> thing
> for
> the
> disciples
> was
> that
> Jesus
> was
> there
> in
> the
> midst
> of
> the
> wind
> and
> storm!

The wonderful thing for the disciples was that Jesus was there in the midst of the wind and storm. During the fourth watch of the night, they suddenly saw Him walking toward them on the sea.

Walking on the sea meant treading on serpents and scorpions, and so it has come to represent total victory for every believer worldwide. A person who can walk on water also has no fear of serpents and scorpions and can *"tread"* on them (see Luke 10:19). If Jesus could walk on the sea, then He could do anything. So walking on the sea represented His dominion (and ours) over the entire Universe. As He put His feet upon that sea, He was treading upon every scorpion and serpent around.

What Peter did when he walked on water was very different from what Jesus did when He walked on the sea.

Peter was not required to walk on the *"sea,"* as Jesus did. He was simply required to walk on *"water."* What this means is that what Jesus did encompassed all of humanity. Peter only walked on water. He was not required to save the whole world.

The water we are required to walk on is our particular sphere of influence in the world. The Lord will take care of the rest of the *"sea."*

A TROUBLING EXPERIENCE

And when the disciples saw him walking on the sea, they were troubled, saying, It is a spirit; and they cried out for fear.

Matthew 14:26, KJV

The powerful storms that arose suddenly and without much advance warning on the Sea of Galilee were terrifying to the local fishermen. The winds that blew down from the surrounding mountains were extremely forceful at times, and once they hit the sea, they whipped up massive waves. As a result, many fishermen had lost their lives, and so, seeing Jesus walking on the water frightened the disciples because they thought it was the spirit of one of those who had died in such a storm

When the Lord visits us, the experience is often troubling. We can't understand it, because it's beyond the realm of our thinking. Therefore it frightens us, and we are in danger of missing its benefits because we have not discerned the presence of the Lord.

Sometimes we have great difficulty discerning what is and what is not the manifestation of God's Spirit, and therefore we are again in danger of missing His best for our lives. There Jesus was walking on the sea, and His own disciples didn't recognize Him. They thought it was a spirit, and possibly even an evil spirit.

Many times, when winds are blowing against us, and God begins to do something very unusual, we think it's coming from the devil, and we actually begin to rebuke it. *This can't be from God,* we're thinking. But it was indeed Jesus; they just hadn't recognized Him. And the same is often true of us today.

Rather than receive Jesus with rejoicing, the disciples *"cried out for fear."* We can understand how they felt. We are also seeing things that we've never seen before, and it isn't always easy to discern that it is, indeed, a visitation from God.

Jesus Calmed their Fears and Caused Peter to Walk on Water

But straightway Jesus spake unto them, saying, Be of good cheer; it is I; be not afraid. And Peter answered him and said, Lord, if it be thou, bid me come unto thee on the water.

And he [Jesus] said, Come.
And when Peter was come out of the ship,
he walked on the water, to go to Jesus.
Matthew 14:27-29, KJV

This all happened on the Sea of Galilee, one of the deepest spots on the face of the earth, as noted early on in the book. There God called Peter by name and urged him to get out of the ship, put his feet on the water, and start walking in a way he had never walked before. I like that, and I feel the call of God today to do the same.

PETER'S ENCOUNTER WITH THE DEEP

When Jesus called him to walk on water, these were, in one sense of the word, uncharted waters for him. He had never walked on water before. Jesus knew this, but He was calling Peter to the unknown.

In another sense, Peter knew these waters well. He had fished them every single day of his adult life. He was, after all, a fisherman of Galilee. There was not an inch of the shore of that great lake and not an area of water, shallow or deep, that he didn't know. But this day the waters were somehow very different. With one call from the Lord, the familiar waters had become charged with the miraculous, and they were no longer familiar to him. He had never been this way before, and just one simple call from the Lord would suddenly thrust him into his destiny.

Through that one call, the Lord would bring Peter to total victory over the deep. These were uncharted waters, but they held purpose for Peter's life. Move on out into your deeper waters.

This New Visitation

We are experiencing a mighty visitation of God in the Church today, and Jesus is standing in the midst of us, calling us into the deep. Until now, many of us haven't known that it was Him. We haven't recognized that the day of our visitation is upon us (see 1 Peter 2:12).

Jesus has His hand extended to you right now, and He's calling to you to get out of the ship and to start walking on water. He will not ask you to conquer the whole world; that's His job. He's walking on the sea. All you have to do is walk on your spot of water.

Your walk on water will be in the proportion to God's call on your life, and He always empowers us to fulfill the call He places upon us.

Peter must have been trembling with excitement in that moment. He was being called to the deep to see the wonders of God. He jumped out of the ship and immediately began walking on water.

FEAR CAN HINDER US IN THE DEEP

Before Peter had gotten very far, however, fear overcame him:

> *But when he saw the wind boisterous, he was afraid; and beginning to sink, he cried, saying, Lord, save me. And immediately Jesus stretched forth his hand, and caught him, and said unto him, O thou of little faith, wherefore didst thou doubt? And when they were come into the ship, the wind ceased. Then they that were in the ship came and worshipped Him, saying, Of a truth thou art the Son of God.* Matthew 14:30-33, KJV

When the disciples suddenly declared that Jesus was the Son of God, it was not just their own idea. They had received revelation knowledge of who He was. This is what God is wanting to do for every one of us today. The new revelation of who Jesus is in our lives will go far beyond our present level of understanding and experience, but it will come to us only when we get into deeper waters. Having a new revelation of Jesus and experiencing His wonders go together.

Get Onboard for the Great Adventure

In case you haven't figured it out yet, we're on a great adventure with the Lord. Get ready, for God is about to move in ways that we can't even imagine at this present time. We're on the edge of a great new wave of His glory.

In our own meetings and in our personal lives, God has begun to do some very new and exciting things. It was not that we expected these things, for we haven't always known what to expect. It was not that we prayed for them, for we could not have always known what to ask for. And it was not that we have been seeking these particular manifestations, but because He is releasing His glory in the earth in a whole new way.

This current wave is greater than the wave we experienced just last year, and we are receiving testimonies from other pastors and Christian leaders describing the very same thing. They were not looking for these particular manifestations either. They just started happening, by the grace and mercy of God.

In Jesus' day, it all happened because of the disciples response to His constraining arm. Lose your fear of His constraints, and soon you, too, will be seeing *His Wonders in the Deep.*

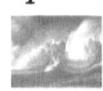

Chapter 13

"The Spirit of the Lord Is Upon Me"

The Spirit of the Lord God is upon me, because the Lord has anointed and qualified me to preach the Gospel of good tidings to the meek, the poor and afflicted; He has sent me to bind up and heal the brokenhearted, to proclaim liberty to the [physical and spiritual] captives and the opening of the eyes to those who are bound.

Isaiah 61:1

This may be the most "claimed" portion of scripture in the entire Bible, and many of you who are reading this have probably claimed it at some point as a *rhema* word for your own life.

1

If ever there was a scripture passage with the sound of destiny upon it, this is it.

Still, today, this remarkable passage of scripture resounds with a clarion call that cannot be denied or refused. It echoes with a sound that urges you to become what you have been called to become from the foundations of the earth, to leave the safety of the shallow waters and launch out into the deep.

I hear the cry of destiny, the cry of Heaven, the sound of the Kingdom, ringing through these words, and I trust that you do too.

Jesus' Early Ministry

At one point, fairly early in His ministry on earth, Jesus was traveling around the Galilee, preaching in the synagogues and being honored and praised by all who heard Him. When He came to Nazareth, where He had been brought up, He went to the synagogue on the Sabbath, for that was His custom. In each service in the synagogues of that day, some honored person was called upon to read the sacred scrolls, and that day Jesus was afforded this honor. Luke recorded what happened next:

And there was handed to Him [the roll of] the book of the prophet Isaiah. He opened (unrolled) the book and found the place where it was written. The Spirit of the Lord [is] upon Me ... .

Luke 4:17-18

There was something very strategic about this moment, but it did not happen accidentally. As Jesus stood there in the synagogue of His hometown, He was not able to just pick any scripture to read. He must open to and read the next passage in order. Anyone picking up the scroll to read it that day would have read the very same passage. It was simply the reading of the day. But what Jesus was reading was powerful, and it was pertinent to His present situation:

The Spirit of the Lord [is] upon Me, because He has anointed Me [the Anointed One, the Messiah] to preach the good news (the Gospel) to the poor; He has sent Me to announce release to the captives and recovery

I hear the cry of destiny, the cry of Heaven, the sound of the Kingdom, ringing through these words, and I trust that you do too!

3

*of sight to the blind, to send forth as de-
livered those who are oppressed [who
are downtrodden, bruised, crushed, and
broken down by calamity], to proclaim the
accepted and the acceptable year of the
Lord [the day when salvation and the free
favors of God profusely abound]. Then He
rolled up the book and gave it back to the
attendant and sat down; and the eyes of all
in the synagogue were gazing [attentively]
at Him. And He began to speak to them:
Today this Scripture has been fulfilled
while you are present and hearing.*

Luke 4:18-21

What Jesus was saying was so wonderfully
profound. He was not only saying that He was the
fulfillment of the Scriptures; He was also saying that
He was the Grand Jubilee established by Moses:

*And you shall hallow the fiftieth year and
proclaim liberty throughout all the land to
all its inhabitants. It shall be a jubilee for
you; and each of you shall return to his an-
cestral possession [which through poverty
he was compelled to sell], and each of you
shall return to his family [from whom he was
separated in bond service]. That fiftieth year
shall be a jubilee for you; in it you shall not
sow, or reap and store what grows of itself,*

4

or gather the grapes of the uncultivated vines. Leviticus 25:10-11

For Jews, Jubilee was the year following seven cycles of seven years each, and during that very special year, all debts were forgiven, all slaves were freed, and all land was allowed to rest. It was a year of great rejoicing.

Jesus is our Great Jubilee. Through Him, *"the free favors of God profusely abound"* to us all.

Our Lord Jesus is the year of favor, and He came to proclaim the year of the favor of the Lord. To walk in the anointing of Isaiah 61 is to live in Jubilee and in the favor of the Lord, to walk in the deeper waters that we have been called to. Jubilee comes in order to release an anointing that can cause us to preach the Gospel to the poor, set the captives free, cause blind eyes to open, the lame to walk and the deaf to hear.

We don't have to wait another fifty years to experience Jubilee. Today, this very moment, you can experience your greatest Jubilee. This is the time for it. This is the set time for the favor of the Lord to come upon you. This is the set time to experience the anointing of Isaiah 61, to walk in the anointing that Jesus came into the world to release, to launch out into the deep and let down your nets for a draught.

In
this
hour,
Jesus
will
do
His
ministering
to
the
meek,
the
poor
and
the
afflicted
(the
sea
of
humanity
all
around
us)
through
us!

This is the day, and this is the hour, the set time of the Lord, for your Jubilee, for Your Grand Jubilee has come. He, Jesus, wants to minister to you and, then, He wants to minister to others through you.

JESUS' CALL

Every prophetic word and vision that came forth from our Lord form part of a picture. If we can get enough of the pieces of that picture into place, we will have a better understanding of just what He is trying to show us. We are living in evil days, and this world is out of control. Despite that fact, God has chosen certain times to do great things. And this, I'm sure, is one of those days. At the right moment, you will have a sensing that the time is right for you. You are destined to reach men and women sitting in deepest darkness. Like Jesus in the time He walked upon the earth, you will feel the Spirit of the Lord God upon you.

Look at this passage again. He said, *"The Spirit of the Lord God is upon me, because the Lord has anointed and qualified me to preach the Gospel of good tidings to the meek, the poor, and afflicted"* (Isaiah 61:1). This was a picture of Jesus. He is our Jubilee, but it is also a picture of us. In this hour, Jesus will do His ministering to the meek, the poor and the afflicted (the sea of humanity all around us) through us.

We don't always have a keenness and an understanding of what God is doing for us. Whatever else is happening in our lives, we can know that this is the day the Lord has made, and we can rejoice and be glad in it. Our destiny is to carry out the ministry of Jesus. This is the reason we were called from the foundations of the world. He came to save the lost, and now He has made us the lights of the world.

Like Jesus, we can say: *"He has sent me to bind up and heal the brokenhearted, to proclaim liberty to the [physical and spiritual] captives"* (Isaiah 61:1). God's Word was clearly speaking of Jesus, but it is also speaking of us today. We, too, are called to bind up and heal the brokenhearted and to proclaim liberty. It's your time.

7

A Very Special Day

Today is a very special day, set apart just for you and for me. It's a divinely-ordered day, not an evil day. It's a blessed day, an anointed day, a glorious day. God has brought it about because of what He has planned for you in the very near future.

His blessing is right around the corner. The very next step you take and the very next breath you breathe are critical. This next hour before you, this next day, this next month, this next year are all divinely ordered. Your footsteps have been ordained by God with a special purpose.

By His Spirit, God wants to affirm to you today that the Spirit of the Lord God is upon you. He has anointed you to preach the Gospel to the poor, to go to the nations, to set at liberty those who are in captivity, to open the blind eyes. Those who are lame will walk. Those who cannot hear will hear. The same anointing that was upon Jesus is now upon you.

Like Jesus, you can say: *"To proclaim the acceptable year of the Lord [the year of His favor] ..."* (Isaiah 61:2). Again, this speaks of Jubilee, and when it comes, He will do all that He has said He will do.

So it's time *"to proclaim"* it. What are we *"to proclaim"*? That this is your year, the year of God's favor upon your life and ministry. You are in the timing of the Lord. You are favored of Him. He is your Grand Jubilee, and He is about to loose upon you the fullness of what He has prepared for your life. That should excite every single one of you.

What Is this Day of Vengeance of Our God?

Jesus also said: *"And the day of vengeance of our God ..."* (Isaiah 61:2). When God poured out His Spirit in the Pensacola Revival, that place became a fountainhead of spiritual activity for the nation and even for much of the world. I went there as often as I possibly could. There we sang a song that spoke of the vengeance of God. It was unusual because the mentality of the Church to that point had been, "Watch out! God's going to smite you. His vengeance is about to come down upon you." But when God spoke of the day of His vengeance, He coupled it with *"the year of His favor."* I'm God's favorite child, and your are too. You're the blessed of God, the seed of Abraham. You're a joint heir with Jesus Christ. That means that He's your elder Brother, and you're in line for throneship because of it. What's His is yours because it comes right down the line.

So when God speaks of the day of His vengeance, what does He mean? It's not vengeance against you. It means that He will avenge you of everything that comes against you, every-thing that tries to oppress you. This is the day of God's favor upon your life, and part of that favor is the manifestation of His vengeance against anything that opposes you. So, move on out into deeper waters. What are you wait-ing for?

Why is what I am writing here true? Because the Spirit of the Lord is upon you. Because He's anointed you to preach the Gospel to the poor, to cause the blind to see, to set at liberty those who are bound in prisons and in chains. The lame shall walk, the blind shall see, the deaf shall hear. The year of God's favor and the day of His vengeance are all part of the same blessing.

God's vengeance is even now being loosed against every demonic power that has risen against you to hurt you, to wound you, to cripple you. His vengeance is not against *you*. To the contrary; it is *for* your benefit, as God's beloved child.

If you can get this revelation into your spirit, it will set your free. It will cause you to walk in a liberty you've never experienced until now. You need to know that you're anointed. You're the favored of God. You have a destiny upon you, and you can walk into that destiny without fearing what the devil might do.

BE ASSURED OF GOD'S LOVE

Christians have gotten into the habit of picking-ing and choosing which of God's promises they want to receive. Many say, "Oh, God, I want Your favor, but I surely don't want Your vengeance." When people say that, it's an indication that they've been so beat up, so defeated, so oppressed, so pushed down, so broken — and it has happened so many times — that they're no longer even sure if the Lord loves them or not.

Let me assure you that He does. His favor is upon your life, and His anger is toward your enemies. He will call all those who do you harm in any way to justice. They will pay for hurting or trying to hurt one of God's favored children.

Your heavy burden is about to roll away and be replaced by garments of praise!

BACK TO ISAIAH 61:2 AGAIN

Let's look at Isaiah 61:2 one more time:
To proclaim the acceptable year of the Lord

[the year of His favor] and the day of venge-
ance of our God, to comfort all who mourn.
                                    Isaiah 61:2

Have you ever mourned? I'm sure you have, but soon you will be able to comfort others who mourn. Isaiah continued:

To grant [consolation and joy] to those who
mourn in Zion — to give them an ornament
(a garland or diadem) of beauty instead of
ashes, the oil of joy instead of mourning,
the garment [expressive] of praise instead
of a heavy, burdened, and failing spirit —
that they may be called oaks of righteous-
ness [lofty, strong, and magnificent, distin-
guished for uprightness, justice and right
standing with God], the planting of the Lord,
that He may be glorified. Isaiah 61:3

If you are born again, you are part of Zion, and very soon beauty will replace your ash heap. Your heavy burden is about to roll away and be replaced by garments of praise. You will then be called *"oaks of righteousness."* This means that God will place an anointing upon your broken life and make something beautiful of it.

So get ready to reach out to hurting and crippled people around you. Get ready to find them in life's highways and byways. God is making you a mighty oak so that you can extend a healing hand to others.

You may feel inadequate, but the anointing upon you will change the situations of those you find in need. Because of your intervention, everything about their lives will turn around.

When God looks at you, He sees something *"lofty, strong, and magnificent, distinguished for uprightness, justice and right standing with God."* You are *"the planting of the Lord,"* and your destiny is to bring Him glory. Why, then, would you linger in shallow places? Step on out.

We Will Suffer Afflictions

The Scriptures don't hide the fact that we will suffer *"afflictions,"* *"fiery darts,"* and every other type of *"persecution"* in this life. Truthfully it doesn't seem right to us that God's children should have to endure these things, but there's always a reason for the things God does or the things He allows. When you are delivered from any affliction, God is glorified, and He deserves all the glory.

One will offer up a song of thanksgiving and then another and another, until we have all joined in great rejoicing. This is miraculous because we were all once so beat up, bruised and oppressed that all we could do was sit on our ash heap and mourn. Now, as we come out of our affliction, we come out with rejoicing — dozens, hundreds, thousands, millions — and we all do the same thing: glorify the Lord who has delivered us. What a sight to behold!

Why are you going through what you are presently going through? Because eventually it will bring glory to God. When you come out of it, He will be glorified. So move on out and start experiencing *His Wonders in the Deep.*

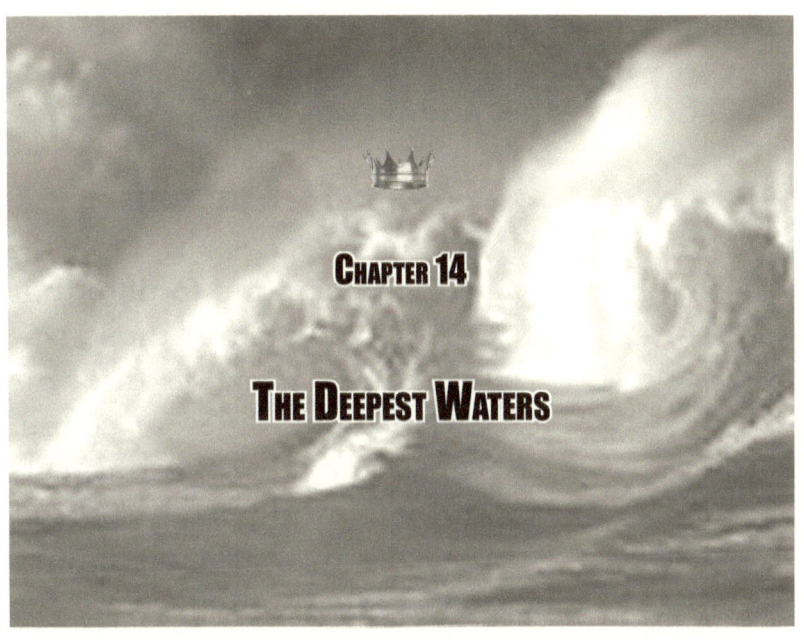

CHAPTER 14

THE DEEPEST WATERS

Then he [my guide] brought me again to the door of the house [of the Lord — the temple], and behold, waters issued out from under the threshold of the temple toward the east, for the front of the temple was toward the east; and the waters came down from under, from the right side of the temple, on the south side of the altar.   Ezekiel 47:1

When Ezekiel had his great vision of the waters issuing forth from under the threshold of the door of the temple, at first that water was ankle deep, then it was knee deep, and then loin deep. As the prophet remained willing to go deeper, the waters continued to deepen, until what had begun as a trickle had now become a mighty river that he could not cross over. The waters, which had begun so simply, were now majestic, glorious, and powerful.

The Fish in the Waters

The deeper Ezekiel went, the more God's anointing intensified on him!

It's interesting to note that Ezekiel saw fish in those waters. They were of different varieties and different colors. These speak of the harvest, and it's an important part of the revealing of God's glory today. We want to feel and see His glory and to witness His signs and wonders, and that's all well and good. But there's a greater purpose to it all. Being called into the deep and to a place of seeing God's wonders is for the purpose of bringing in the great last-day harvest.

The deeper Ezekiel went, the more God's anointing intensified on him. He saw the Shekinah glory of God. Then he experienced an angelic visitation and many other marvelous things.

One of the most important things we need to see regarding Ezekiel's experiences is that, as this great anointing issued out from the temple and the waters got deeper and deeper, the prophet was carried further and further away from the temple. This speaks to us of evangelism. Some Christians feel that they're not called to evangelism, but they're wrong. We're all called to evangelism, for this is the very heartbeat of God.

The outpouring of God that we're now experiencing is not about you, and it's not about me. It's all about the harvest our Lord desires. When Jesus looked at the fields about Him, He noted that they were *"white for harvesting"* (John 4:35). We have taken this to mean they were ready to be harvested. And they were. But what He said meant much more than that.

THE PERFECTION OF RIPENESS

The fact that the fields were so white lets us know that they were very ripe, and if they were not quickly harvested, the fruit would be lost.

There is a perfection of ripeness, and when crops are left longer than the perfect time, they begin to rot on the stalk or vine. We all love to eat ripe things, but few of us enjoy eating something that is overly ripe. Perfect ripeness, then, is a very dangerous state for any crop. If someone doesn't gather it in quickly, it will die on the stalk and be forever lost.

This explains the urgent call to the deep we are experiencing today. Start walking in the anointing. Start swimming on out into new rivers. Learn to flow with God's currents, and let Him carry you into the deeper places, for souls hang in the balance.

THOSE DEEPEST OF WATERS

As noted earlier, when Ezekiel the prophet saw the water beginning to pour forth from the temple, it began as a mere trickle, but even that trickle had power in it. Everywhere it went — whether it was just a trickle, whether it was ankle deep, knee deep, loin deep, or if it was rivers to swim in — it brought forth life and healing. Whatever was touched by that water was changed.

In the temple itself, great things happened. The very Shekinah glory of God appeared, and God wants to do these same things for us today. We have experienced a cloud of God's presence coming into our meetings many times in recent years, and I love it. Oh, how I love to be in God's glory. I love to be somewhere that He is being praised and worshiped, where we can feel the presence of angels and see the glory of the Father. I love to be where His great and mighty things are happening. It doesn't take much. Just a trickle can bring forth marvelous signs and wonders.

In Ezekiel's revelation, the healing that took place as a result of the waters going forth did not happen at the temple itself. It happened as the waters flowed out or *"issued out"* (KJV), and the deepest part of the water was not found at the temple itself. The further the water flowed from the temple, the deeper it got. What does this mean to us today? If you really want to swim in some deep waters, then go to some of the Third-World countries. Go where no one else wants to go. Get out into God's great harvest fields, and begin to reap for Him. Hear His heart today. As you respond to His call, He will show you His wonders.

ALREADY WHITE FOR HARVESTING

If you want to know the Father's heart today, lift up your eyes and look on His fields. He said they were *"already white for harvesting."* Again, the fields are *"white,"* meaning they are at their peak and are in danger of perishing. When that is true, one more day's delay can be disastrous. One more day's delay can mean death and destruction.

Those fields are not just ready; they are more than ready. Souls are dying! Hear their cry and understand the Father's heart for them. The psalmist declared:

*Ask of Me, and I will give you the nations as
Your inheritance, and the uttermost parts of
the earth as Your possession.* Psalm 2:8

When we think of a desirable spiritual inheritance, we often imagine that it will be righteousness, peace, and joy in the Kingdom of God. But our inheritance is much greater than that; it is to be *"the nations."*

Do you want to know God's heartcry today? It is for souls. He *"greatly love{s} and dearly prize{s} the world":*

*For God so greatly loved and dearly prized
the world that He [even] gave up His only
begotten (unique) Son, so that whoever believes in (trusts in, clings to, relies on) Him
shall not perish (come to destruction, be lost)
but have eternal (everlasting) life.*
John 3:16

As much as we love to gather together with other saints to worship God, to share our testimonies of God's goodness, and to see God's glory displayed, the really deep waters exist where His glory flows out to the nations, to the needy, to the people sitting in darkness. As we gather together, we may feel His touch upon us, and our spines will tingle, and goose bumps will appear, but the further we can get from the temple, the deeper the waters will become.

The very best blessings in God, therefore, come to us when we are out fulfilling the Great Commission, when we are out doing what He has called us to do — telling others of His love, declaring His goodness among the nations, winning the lost to Him.

Say, "Yes, Lord!"

Saying, "Yes, Lord," to God's call to the nations and then allowing the Spirit of the Lord to thrust us out into deeper waters is the answer we've all been waiting for. It's not enough to have a trickle of water around our toes. It's not enough to be ankle deep, knee deep, or even loin deep. We desperately need rivers to swim in, and those rivers are found among the nations!

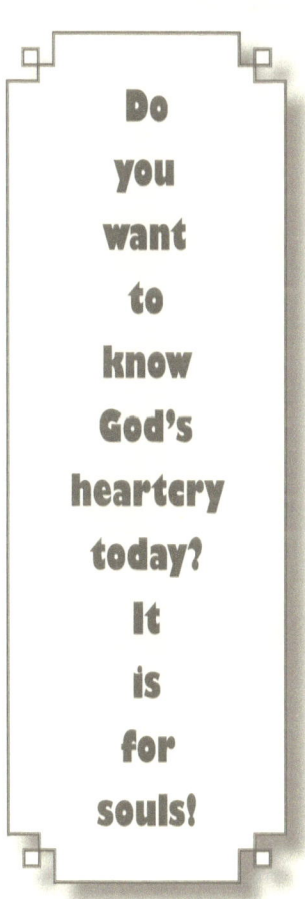

Do you want to know God's heartcry today? It is for souls!

The very purpose for the favor of God upon us, the very purpose for His Jubilee, the very purpose for the promise of Isaiah 61 is that we would be anointed to become a great and powerful army that will go throughout the land, bringing the fires of revival to those who still need to hear. God wants to give you the nations of the world as an inheritance; that's His will for your life today. He's just waiting for you to know *His Wonders in the Deep*.

CHAPTER 15

THIS IS YOUR DAY

This is the day which the LORD hath made;
we will rejoice and be glad in it.
                                    Psalm 118:24, KJV

Several years ago, when I was ministering in a conference along the famous Chesapeake Bay in Maryland, the Lord began to give me new insights into this very familiar and beloved portion of scripture.

These are prophetic words, and God's Spirit must quicken them to our spirits. Many of us have memorized them. We have sung them, we have claimed them, and we have declared them. Often we have done this in the midst of some difficult circumstances. But when God spoke to me, the verse suddenly took on a whole new dimension. I love how the Amplified Bible says it:

This is the day which the Lord has brought about; we will rejoice and be glad in it.

God *"brought about"* this day and this circumstance, and when He did, He had something wonderful in mind. Rejoice in that fact.

The book of Revelation also speaks of rejoicing in our present circumstances:

Let us rejoice and shout for joy [exulting and triumphant]! Let us celebrate and ascribe to Him the glory and honor, for the marriage of the Lamb [at last] has come, and His bride has prepared herself. Revelation 19:7

Here the Lord was speaking of a specific time, a set hour, and a set day, and I believe this day and this hour are upon us.

His Bride Has Prepared Herself

"His bride has prepared herself." Are you preparing yourself? God has dropped into the spirits of many of us a desire to be ready for that day at all costs.

2

What are we preparing for? We must prepare ourselves for a new move of God. We must prepare ourselves for a breakthrough in our personal lives and ministries. We must prepare ourselves for a bursting forth of our giftings and callings. This is our time. God said it, and I believe it.

Psalm 118:24 carries a parallel theme. It also speaks of a day and hour in which the Bride has made herself ready. In the wording of the psalm, the Bride is making herself ready for the King of Glory. She is preparing herself so that she can be an instrument through which revival can flow. In her preparation, she is cleansing herself, sanctifying herself, and consecrating her life. She does this with great urgency and excitement, for the day is at hand.

God "brought about" this day and this circumstance, and when He did, He had something wonderful in mind.

3

Now! Today!

The promise of this psalm is not just something that we should declare when we are feeling downtrodden. We must receive the revelation that this is the day that the Lord has brought about. This is the day of His favor, this is the day of His blessing, this is the day of renewal, or revival, this is the day of His glory being revealed in the earth, this is the day that the Lord has brought about for this generation. How exciting!

This is the hour, so we must cross over and possess all that is ours. Every wall of Jericho will come down. The walls that have kept you out and obstacles that have prevented you from possessing what is rightfully yours are coming down, and you can go in and possess your promise.

This special day which the Lord has brought about is a wonderful one, and therefore we must rejoice in it. In this light, the passage takes on a whole new meaning. We are not just rejoicing to get ourselves out of some depressing situation. We are rejoicing because we have knowledge and revelation of what this day is all about, because of the fact that God has supernaturally brought it about and because we are right here in the middle of it. Praise God! No wonder we are to rejoice!

WAITING FOR HEAVEN

Many of us can't wait to get to Heaven and talk to the patriarchs and Moses, and Elijah. We women can't wait to see Esther, Deborah, and Ruth. We have in our minds a picture of us going to seek them out. But I believe that all of these Old Testament saints will be at the gates of Heaven waiting to welcome us as we arrive because I'm convinced that what will happen on the earth in our time will be greater than the events of the past. Yes, we will see our Red Sea parting, out walls of Jericho falling, and the multitude being fed by the multiplication of a few loaves and fishes. Jesus Himself tells us that greater works will be done:

I assure you, most solemnly I tell you, if anyone steadfastly believes in Me, he will himself be able to do the things that I do; and he will do even greater things than these, because I go to the Father.

John 14:12

It is not wrong to long for Heaven. We all want to experience its realms of glory, but I believe that we are standing in realms of glory right here and right now on the earth. Those who have gone on to Heaven would love to be here experiencing what we are now experiencing. They would love to be standing with us in this glory.

This Is the Day

This is the day which the Lord has brought about. It is a day like no other day. This is not just a normal day, and we are not led to praise the Lord for a regular day just to help us get through it somehow. No! A thousand times no! This is the most awesome and wonderful day the Lord has given us the privilege to live in, and that's what we're rejoicing about. This is a blessed day, an anointed day, a dynamic day, a glorious day, and He has brought it about because of what He has planned for our lives.

His plans and purposes are very near. They're just around the corner; it could come with the next step you take or the next breath you breathe. The Lord is divinely ordering your footsteps, and He wants to affirm to you today that the Spirit of the Lord God is upon you. This is the day that He has brought about for you to experience *His Wonders in the Deep*.

CHAPTER 16

IT'S TIME, MY FRIEND

Some go down to the sea and travel over it in ships to do business in great waters; these see the works of the Lord and His wonders in the deep. Psalm 107:23-24

My friend, you have begun to do business in deep waters, and you must never return to the shallows. If you want to see the wonders of God, there is no other way. There are many things that we have not yet seen or experienced, and God wants to pull back the veil from our eyes so that we can see them and experience them.

We have seen what it means to be launched into the deep. Perhaps we should think also on what it does not mean.

What It Does Not Mean

Have you felt recently like your courage was melting away?

Launching forth does not mean that you will always sail on calm seas:

For he commands and raises up the stormy wind, which lifts up the waves of the sea. [Those aboard] mount up to the heavens.
Psalm 107:25-26

Storms will come. Rains will fall. Lightening bolts will strike. Thunder will crash. Winds and waves will rage. But in the midst of it all, those who have gone into the deep to do business for the Lord will not falter. They may indeed experience moments of fear and feel that they are at their wits end, but they shall *"mount up to the heavens."*

Have you felt recently like your courage was melting away?

Their courage melts away because of their plight. They reel to and fro and stagger like a drunken man, and are at their wit's end [all their wisdom has come to nothing]. Then they cry to the Lord in their trouble, and He brings them out of their distresses.

Psalm 107:26-28

That's His promise. *"He brings them out of their distresses."* Stand firm on that promise.

You've Been Drafted

By now you've seen that when the Lord thrusts you out into the deep, it's not a request or an option. You are being drafted. If you haven't yet received your draft notice, get ready. It's coming. You are being enlisted, not exactly voluntarily, but at the order of the Lord of Hosts. Embrace that privilege.

You may have been living in very shallow waters, playing it safe, but something is changing. Your draft notice is in the mail. Get ready for serious service to the Kingdom.

When I was still a teenager, the Vietnam War broke out, and suddenly young men all around me were being drafted. It didn't matter who they were or what they were doing, if they were of draft age, they were in immediate danger of being called up.

3

Suddenly, all of the young men were scrambling to get into college, hoping in that way to avoid the draft. Some even left the country and fled to Canada when their notice came and they were not prepared to answer the call. Their number had come up, and they were not ready. Is your number next? Are you ready to answer God's call?

This word *draft* has several meanings. It can mean military conscription, but it can also refer to a catch of fish, as it was used in the Bible (with different spelling — *draught*). Get ready for your draught.

Draft can also mean a bank note, and I believe that is also applicable these days. When God calls you, He will have provision ready for you. Your draft is in the mail. Thank God for His provision.

Just a Speck on the Horizon?

Compared to the larger plan of God being birthed in the earth right now, you and I may be just a speck on the horizon. God's plan is huge, and it takes in all of humanity. His plan is for revival in the whole earth, a loosing of a great river of anointing. But that doesn't make your part in it or my part in it any less important.

Get ready to serve. Just as a baby dropping into the birth canal signifies the nearness of its birth, there are many signals all around us that God is about to do some amazing things for us

4

souls yet to come into the Kingdom are brought into relationship with their King. That fact determines all priorities in the Kingdom, and God wants to show us His heart in this respect today.

It's time, my friend, to move on out and experience *His Wonders in the Deep.*

Let's begin asking, for God is ready to do miracles for us. He's just waiting for us to get connected to the fullness of the great I AM. It's time.

I can declare (and I often do it publicly) that there is not a single petition that I have written down and presented to the Lord that He has not answered. Write yours down too, and then take that paper and present it to the Lord. Wave it before Him by faith. Lay hands on it and declare the thing you have petitioned to be done. Believe the Lord to answer you. And, of course, do it all in the name of Jesus.

God Is Mindful of You

God is very mindful of you today. He is mindful of you as an individual, He is mindful of you as a family, and He is mindful of you as a local church. He is mindful of everything that concerns us, and this is true for every single inhabitant upon the face of the earth today.

The heartbeat of God is not only for you or for your particular circle of friends and family members; His heart beats for something much larger, He is touched for the nations. If we can only begin to get closer to His bosom, we will more clearly hear His heartcry.

There can be no doubt that we are now living in the last days, but the consummation of the ages will not transpire until the harvest of

EPILOGUE

My launch into the deep is not yet a completed work in any sense of the word. Each new day brings fresh challenges in this regard. God's will for each of us is never stagnation. He has ordained that we conquer new territory periodically, and that keeps our spiritual lives ever fresh and new.

Yesterday was yesterday, and today is a new day. So launch out into the deep and let down your nets for a draught.

I have put a lot of emphasis upon evangelism, for that is the heartbeat of the Father, but it is my desire for you to understand that *His Wonders in the Deep* entails much more than evangelism, or gathering in the harvest. Along with that will be many magnificent workings of Heaven. Stepping out into the deep will enable you to experience the miraculous, great healings, and marvelous signs and wonders. Your eyes will behold the manifestations of God's glory. The windows of Heaven will be opened over you, and Hcaven's display will be your portion. Revelation of the Word will become yours, and the deeper things of God will manifest in your life.

As we have seen, there are many wondrous things that we don't yet know of just waiting for us to discover. I pray that you have been challenged through this book to search out and find *His Wonders in the Deep.*

Author Contact Page

You may contact Andy McDougal in any of the following ways:

18896 Greenwell Springs Road
Greenwell Springs, LA 70739

AndysMinistry@gmail.com

www.facebook.com/andrea.mcdougal.3
www.facebook.com/andymcdougalministries

Phone 225-572-9844

THE GLORY OF GOD REVEALED

The What, the Why and the How of the Current Revival of Signs and Wonders

Andrea "Andy" McDougal

YOUR Camels *Are Coming*

The Bride's Journey
to
Destiny

Andrea "Andy" McDougal

The *ARROWS* *of the* *LORD*

Andrea "Andy" McDougal

The

Power

of the

Seed

Andrea "Andy" McDougal

A Southern Lady's Tea Journey

A Legacy

Andrea "Andy" McDougal

A Southern Lady's Tea Adventures

Andrea "Andy" McDougal